Wizz Kid

Brian Davey

To everyone who has been afraid and has survived.

To all the kids, young and old who have learnt responsibility, consequences and self confidence through using what you cannot see to get to where you want to go, this is for you. To all those who are starting the adventure… enjoy the journey.

I need to acknowledge the support of the people who have helped make this happen. My loving and patient wife who shares my love of sailing and who encouraged me to write and publish this story. My three wonderful children who have all grown up to be proficient sailors and the other the kids that I have coached to sail. Janet McKenzie Jeans for creating the cover and my patient editor, Dr Linda Gibson-Langford who challenged my ideas and helped the story to flow.

Activity on the deck returned to the tasks at hand. The sailors fidgeted with ropes, cables, masts and shackles as they prepared their dinghies for the day's race.

All activity stopped again! This time it was the captain of *Wave Leaper* - Old Crusty a name inherited over the years. Ignoring everybody, he staggered through the throng, dragging his gammy leg. Pushing past anyone in his way, he moved toward the jetty on the western side of the Sailing Club where his tender was tied. He carried a week's worth of groceries in a battered army rucksack. A couple of carrot tops waved out of the flap.

The last obstacle before reaching the jetty was a sail spread on the ground, blocking Crusty's path. It belonged to Billy. Crusty stopped. Considered his options.

Billy stood defiantly, hands on hips, silently challenging the old man. After a brief hesitation, Old Crusty, left leg limping, sauntered across the sail; his footprints making a wrinkled mess of the smooth sailcloth.

"What did you do that for?" shouted Billy. "You old bugger! Show some respect! Have you no idea what sails are worth? That's right. Show your ignorance!"

ONE

A cheeky handful of wind reached down and tossed Clara's sailing cap onto the deck adjacent to the slipway. It lay there. Just long enough for her to reach down and nearly grab it. But no - it was off again; sliding along, stopping every few metres. After several games of tag, the cap slipped over the side of the deck. Into the water it dropped and, caught by an eddy, swirled back to where Clara could reach over and grab it. The cap, firmly in her grip, was now dripping and floppy, disappointed that it had been treated so badly.

Clara frowned at her soggy hat, her frustration clear to all who had watched and not offered to help.

Clara knew she was different. Despite her earnest application to learn the 'ropes of sailing', despite her being around Banjo Point Sailing Club for over a year, and despite her natural affinity to water, no one had really come to accept Clara as a genuine member of the Sailing Club.

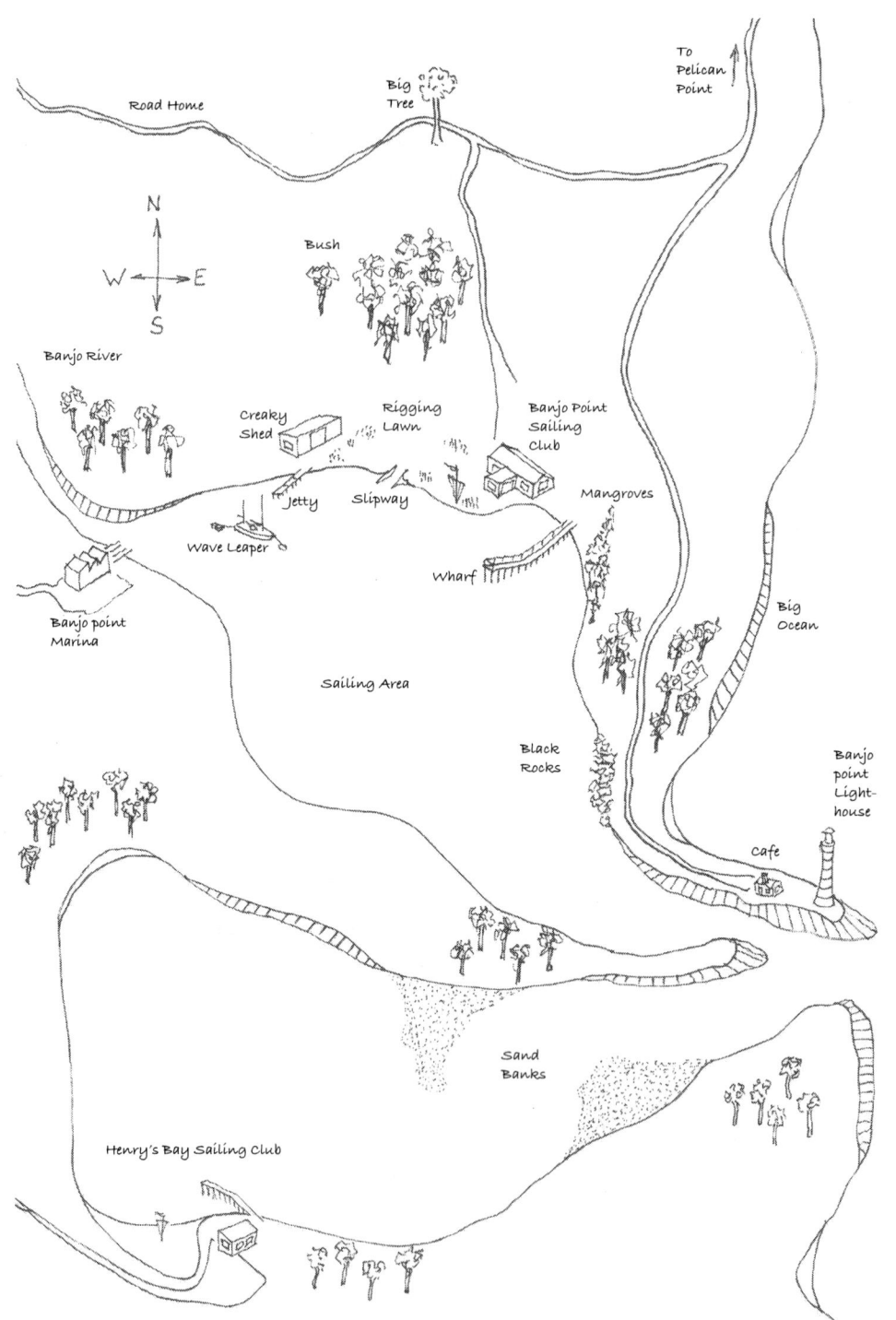

As a final insult, he hollered, "I hope your boat sinks, you old goat."

Crusty, with a glint in his eye, hobbled on.

Sailors, young and old alike, watched in amusement. It was an old feud, one that seemed to escalate each season.

Without warning, a westerly gale swirled down the Banjo River in full force. On the rigging lawn, the younger sailors tried desperately to hold their boats down while keeping their gear under control.

Chaos reigned as masts were dropped and sailors scrambled to place their equipment into the musty darkness of the boat shed. The shed's corrugated iron sides moaning with each strengthening gust from this unexpected westerly.

The members of the Sailing Club knew that westerly winds, in themselves, were rare, but when they arrived, it was always sudden, violent and unexpected. It was a rough day if you were caught out sailing when a westerly descended upon the river, changing the generally calm, safe sailing area into a treacherous environment.

The rigging lawn cleared, the young sailors gathered near the front corner of the clubhouse, swapping stories, laughing about how they had found one of their sails twisted into the back fence of the parking lot, or one of their towels hugging a car's bonnet.

As the wind twisted and whirled around Banjo Point, the Clubhouse, overflowing with members retreating from the gale force winds, buzzed with excitement. The younger sailors huddled into one of the window corners. That is, all but Clara!

She stood back. She wanted to be included, but there always seemed to be a closed circle of shoulders every time she thought of moving forward.

"Hmmm," she shrugged, "I don't need those sorts of friends, anyway."

As the older blokes, the seasoned sailors, settled into the comfortable vintage chairs near the bar, tea and hot pies were being served at the canteen.

The more experienced sailors laughed and joked about the storm, remembering how bad it had been in '68, but especially in '84, when three of the Gremlins had capsized and sunk; the young sailors swimming frantically to safety.

And then Billy gasped. His facial expression changed in a way that stopped the conversation. All eyes followed his gaze.

A mast was passing the front window of the Clubhouse, very close, heading down river as the wind howled its anger. In an instant, everybody was pouring out of the front door. Old Crusty's yacht, *Wave Leaper,* his home - was heading downstream at a rate of knots towards the rocks in the bend of the river. Club members were shouting instructions while the younger sailors scrambled down the wooden stairs near the wharf and onto the river bank.

Old Crusty was standing in the cockpit of his yacht; the tiller across to starboard, willing the boat to turn so that he could gain some control and avoid the rocks. It was obvious that his mooring had broken, and that, clearly, he needed onboard help.

The Sailing Club's rescue boats had been packed away at the onset of the squall. There was no time to relaunch them before *Wave Leaper* would crash onto the jagged black rocks.

Billy, turning to anybody who would listen, grizzled, "Maybe, at last, the old grump will get what he deserves."

*

Clara made a neat splash as she dived off the end of the wharf. In no time, she caught up to the yacht heading towards the sharply protruding black rocks.   Crusty turned towards Clara's shout of "Crussssstttty". Grabbing her arm with a strong firm hand, he hoisted her on board. Within seconds they were making their way to the bow, and, working in unison, deployed the anchor. A heartening splash as the anchor fell was followed by a puff of rusty dust. The anchor chain clattered over the bow roller and into the water.

And then, a miracle. *Wave Leaper* swung around as the chain sprung taught. She faced obediently into the wind; the anchor dug deep into the mud.

*Wave Leaper'*s stern came to rest mere metres from the jagged rocks.

Without looking back, Clara dived over the bow and swam confidently back to the pebbly patch of beach, upstream of the muddy mangrove flats. The wind, still restless, raged through her as she stood up in the shallows; her dripping clothes cold against her skin. Adults and kids gathered around her. Someone wrapped her in a warm towel and walked her back to the Club.

Sitting in front of the large Clubhouse window, a cup of warm chocolate brew in her hand, Clara looked out along the river. The rescued boat, *Wave Leaper,* was still there.

She had saved *Wave Leaper* from the jagged black rocks on the bend. Clara was being hailed as 'hero of the day'. But not everybody was happy with Clara's initiative.

TWO

For Clara, it had been a difficult week. There was a rising tide of anti-Clara feeling at school. Billy had hoped Crusty and his boat, *Wave Leaper*, would be wrecked and that the grumpy old bugger would disappear from Banjo Point, and their lives, forever. Several of the young sailors at school agreed with Billy's rendition of the story, totally disregarding the show of courage and skill that Clara had exhibited. She was determined to ignore their jokes and rude comments, hoping that she would still be appreciated at the Sailing Club.

Saturday raced around again. The land was heating up and the wind, coming off the ocean, just over the line of dunes, was cool and invigorating.

It was a perfect day for sailing. The sun was out and a few puffy clouds skidded across the sky from the northeast

Hoping it would be a good day, a sense of anticipation filled Clara. With the sea breeze freshening, Clara, sailing bag in hand, headed down the hill to Banjo Point Sailing Club. As she looked toward the Clubhouse, she mused over its long brick building, with its decade after decade of disconnected extensions.

It certainly had its own character. Each addition disregarded what had already been built. Ugly as it looked, it was held in loyal regard by members who knew the stories echoed in each of the extensions. The canteen was off to one side with a tiled roof; the bar on the opposite side had a green fibreglass roof, allowing the afternoon sun to play across the tables and chairs. The middle section had green 1970s tables; the plastic chairs, a medley of colours and styles. The dinghy storage locker - affectionately known as the *Creaky Shed* - was to the west on the furthermost side of the rigging lawn.

Despite its shambolic architecture and fittings, the Clubhouse had dignity! The walls were festooned with Honour Boards from every class of boat and every year since 1924 - the year the Banjo Point Sailing Club was opened. Famous names could be seen on many of the Boards: members who had gone on to represent Australia at the Olympics, winning Gold Medals, or became famous for sailing the Sydney to Hobart Yacht Race or even 'around the world' yacht races. There, amongst it all, was the *Gremlin Honour Board* with the inscription **John Brenton 1965 Club Champion.** Rumour had it that

Brenton was Old Crusty, although very few wanted to believe that it was true.

*

As Clara rounded the point to the Clubhouse, she could see that Old Crusty's boat was back on its mooring. The rigging lawn was already packed with sailors, young and old, as she stepped over and around sails and equipment. Selecting an open spot, Clara dumped her sailing bag and headed to the *Creaky Shed* to collect her boat.

A Gremlin, short and stumpy, was a good type of boat for kids learning to sail and race, competitively. Clara's boat, *Wizz Kid*, was old, having been a source of learning by a lot of kids over the years. More importantly, *Wizz Kid* was reputed to be amazingly fast when the wind rose, though few could remember when it last won a race!

Once out in the warm sunlight, Clara quickly *stepped* the mast, laying the lines in place in readiness to hoist the sail.

Something caught her eye. An envelope, sticking out from her rope bag. Carefully she removed it. In neat cursive writing, 'Lifesaving Kid' was written on the front. She turned it over and slipped her skinny finger under the flap, tearing it open.

Pulling out a handwritten note, she read:

"Hi Kid,
Thanks for coming to my rescue last week. You did a brave thing and pulled me out of a rotten mess. Come down any day this coming week and I'll give you a bit of coaching.
We will get Wizz Kid moving fast! I owe you."

And there it was. The signature at the bottom - John (*Wave Leaper*). Clara carefully folded the note, placing it back into the envelope, and stuffed it deeply into her sailing bag.

Clara wasn't sure what to do. She was aware of the importance to get permission before going anywhere with anyone - about being safe. All that she had been told screamed out to her. Be careful! Don't do it!

But she was sensible! Maybe she could slip down to the Clubhouse after school. Be back before Mum came home from her work at the local Post Office. It would still be daylight and at this time of the year, especially on Wednesdays, the Clubhouse was busy with members socialising after a bit of afternoon sailing. Meeting up with Crusty, she decided, would be safe.

Preoccupied with this 'mysterious note', Clara fumbled the rest of the rigging. She could see that other boats had already been launched for the afternoon's race, and knew she was going to struggle.

"Now *I* need to move it," she muttered.

Urging herself into action, Clara rushed toward the slipway. With the sail not properly set, flapping against her face, she tumbled over her own feet, and tripped headlong into the river. *Wizz Kid* bumped down the ramp behind her.

"Damn!" Clara mumbled, shaking her head, as she climbed onto *Wizz Kid*. Despite the boat not being properly rigged, she pushed off, shoving the centreboard down the slot. The other kids were sailing around the start line as Clara caught up, still trying to make final adjustments to her sail.

The starting hooter sounded. Gremlins jockeyed for position as they raced down the river in an attempt to make the most of the freshening sea breeze.

After her haphazard departure from the shore, Clara felt her boat was unusually slow, as if weed was stuck on the rudder or centreboard. It was turning into another disappointing race. Looking down the course, she could see the top mark where the leading boats were turning around for the run back to the Clubhouse - and the finishing line!

"Damn! Damn! Bloody Damn! Billy! Always - always - in the front!" she grumbled. Clara hated his arrogance. However, she admitted, he had confidence and he certainly could sail.

As Billy passed her, he called out, "Yo! Muppet! Pretty stupid thing to save that old goat last week."

Clara looked away, but the insult had bitten into her, It hurt! A wave of anger reddened her freckled face. She resisted the anger welling up inside her, determined that Billy would one day regret his arrogance. Confident that she would beat him at what *he* thought he knew best.

He was wrong about her!

One day she would show him! In her mind's eye, she could see it now. Whatever it took! Yup! Decision made! She would take Crusty on as her coach.

As she nudged *Wizz Kid* alongside the slipway, Clara acknowledged that it had not been a good race. However, she had made some decisions! Firm ones.

Jumping into the water, she was aware, as always, that there was no one around to help her. Other kids had mums and dads waiting, ready to whisk their boats up onto the rigging lawn, helping them to de-rig and to pack up.

Clara undid the halyard and dropped the sail into the boat before nudging the bow up onto the slipway. As she jogged over to get her launching dolly, she smiled to herself.

Her secret plan, hidden deep in her sailing bag, warmed her heart. Despite coming last again, the future was hopeful and she knew it.

THREE

Wednesday afternoon. Finally. School was over for the day. Within seconds, Clara was out of the school gate. Running as fast as she could, school bag stuffed with sailing gear, she was focussed. The Sailing Club was at least two kilometres away and she needed to be far from prying eyes. Out of breath, she rounded the hill and slowed as the Sailing Club came into view.

Bounding down the hill, she tried to work out answers to her recurring questions. How will this happen? How will she alert Old Crusty to her presence? How was he going to coach her?

She had decided that, if she could see no one at the Clubhouse, she would hide in the bushes behind the *Creaky Shed*. Watch. Wait. Be patient.

Nearing the bottom of the hill, she was relieved to see that the Clubhouse door was open. In she walked, strolling past a couple of old blokes sanding their boats and a few others, nestled into lounge chairs, chattering away. She slipped past without being noticed. Out into the bright sunshine of the rigging lawn, she hurried over to the *Creaky Shed*, slipping into the darkness through the side door. Confidently, she unlatched the roller door, sliding it upward.

Would that be enough of a signal for Crusty to make his way across to the jetty?

Standing in the darkness of the shed, she fixed her eyes on *Wave Leaper*, bobbing gently on her mooring. She waited. She understood how valuable this moment of time was.

She was also aware that she had lied to Mum, saying that she was going to try out for the netball team. She looked at her mobile.

"OK. I'll wait five more minutes and then I'll wheel my boat out. Regardless!" she whispered.

After less than three minutes, she became impatient, blatantly picking up her mast and marching out onto the lawn. Striding back to the shed, she wheeled out *Wizz Kid*.

As she hoisted the mast, she sighted a dinghy rowing in towards the jetty. It was Crusty. He slowly climbed the ladder onto the jetty and then hobbled his way across the rigging lawn to where she stood, expectantly, beside her boat.

Crusty was old, that was obvious, but how old? Grey hair. A long thin pigtail. Watery blue eyes and a leathery face - no doubt as a consequence of years around boats. He always appeared to be grumpy and impatient.

Clara stepped back behind her boat as Crusty approached, a little uncertain of his presence.

In a gruff voice, Crusty stated, "So you want to sail faster, do you *yungun'*? Well, let's get started then."

With that, he sat down on the lawn beside *Wizz Kid* and looked out across the river; his legs folded neatly under him, back straight as a pole. Clara stood beside her boat and, like Crusty, looked out across the river.

"Never fight the *wind*. You will always lose," he said in a slow monotone, emphasising wind at each breath, "The *wind* is your friend. It's your best friend. Sometimes the *wind* is your only friend."

And with that he gave a deep sigh as if he felt the last statement deep within him.

He continued, "Except, of course, the boat, but that's different. The boat is not your friend. It's a part of you."

He sighed again and waited as if the gravity of his comment needed time to sink in.

"Don't see it as something separate. Be the boat. Feel it."

With that he moved around onto his knees and slowly, protecting his weakened leg, stood up, asking, "Will you be here next week?" and, without waiting for an answer, he turned and walked towards the jetty.

And then, as if an afterthought, he mumbled over his shoulder, "Be rigged and ready by 4pm."

Clara stood beside her boat wondering if that was it - the lesson? Hardly a coaching session. A bit of mumbling and he was gone. To be fair, at least someone was trying to help her sail and that was better than being ignored. Would she be back next week? For sure!

With half an hour in hand, she busied herself with the Gremlin, checking shackles, bolts and nuts, ropes and cleats.

The sun was reflecting off the river onto the Clubhouse windows and back down onto the lawn. It was time to head home. Walking up the hill from the Club, Crusty's words went around, again and again, in her head.

"The wind is your friend... sometimes your only friend."

"Never fight the wind. You will always lose."

"Be the boat. Feel it."

That made no sense. In fact, Clara decided, none of it did.

Leaning on the front gate, Clara pushed hard. As it creaked open, Clara shook her head at the sagging gate, muttering, "Stupid thing."

She slid the key into the lock. No need. It was open. Her heart sank. "Damn!" she thought.

Shoving her sailing bag quickly into the hall closet, she hoped not to face any questions about her late arrival.

"Hello, Sweetie," Mum called from upstairs.

"Hi, Mum."

"How did the netball trial go?"

"Not sure, Mum," Clara lied, "I don't know if they want me."

"That's ok, Honey. They just don't know what they're missing out on."

"Hey, Mum, why are you home so early."

"Ahh, Sweetie. I finished my tasks - permission 'granted' to come home early," she giggled. "Got a date with a dashing man who is taking me to the movies."

As an afterthought, she called out, "There's leftovers in the fridge for your dinner. It's getting late so get stuck into your homework, OK?"

A tiny lump of *loneliness* squeezed her throat. Mum always did that to her. Leftovers in the 'fridge for Clara while Mum would be out enjoying a fancy meal. Being home alone no longer worried Clara. It happened so often, but eating leftovers was beyond fair.

Shaking her head, Clara shoved Mum's junk from the dining room table. As far as she was concerned, her Mum did not have an organised bone in her body.

She reached into her school bag, pulling out her Maths book. Maths, for Clara, was easy. Only a couple of pages of exercises to complete, but that would be quick. As she was completing the set task, her Mum wandered past, stroked Clara's hair, and wished her a cheery goodnight. Clara was now alone.

Ignoring her Geography homework, Clara headed to her bedroom. She wanted to read Crusty's note once more. Hidden in her drawer of t-shirts and shorts, right at the back where Mum was unlikely to find it, Clara picked up the now somewhat grubby and dog-eared envelope with *Lifesaving Kid* written across its front.

Reading it again, she glowed with a sense of wonderment. What prompted her to make that flash decision to dive into the water? It was as if something magnetic had tugged at her, pushing her to swim toward *Wave Leaper*. She remembered, with Crusty's help, working out how to release the anchor.

And something she did not expect. So many people at the Sailing Club had become a little friendlier since then.

As she mused on that moment, she began to wonder how Crusty knew she sailed *Wizz Kid*. Suppose he would have asked one of the old blokes at the Sailing Club. He probably knew a lot more about what was going on than people gave him credit. After all, he lived on *Wave Leaper* and was always working on her. Someone said he was planning to sail her around the world. Considering his plans had nearly ended very close to home only ten days ago, Clara smiled again at having the courage to jump into the river that day to help him.

Clara took out a pen, adding to Crusty's note his sage advice from today.

Never fight the wind. You will always lose.
The wind is your friend.
Feel the boat. Be part of the boat.

She stopped. She wanted to record Crusty's exact words. Was it *be the boat* or was it *feel part of the boat* or perhaps *feel you are a part of the boat.*

Then she remembered Crusty clearly saying, "The wind is your friend...sometimes your only friend."

She quivered. A tinge of sadness as the words swirled around in her head: words that made her feel even lonelier. Maybe that was how old Crusty felt - lonely!

She tried to imagine being part of the boat. She thought about fighting the sail as the wind tried to blow the boat over. She could see herself holding onto the main sheet with all her might. The wind *could not* be a friend. Yet it wasn't the enemy, either.

It just was. And that was that!

Clara was still holding the note; her mind drifting as she thought about the Sailing Club, Billy, and racing.

Her mobile pinged, bringing her back to reality. A text message. Mum!

"Hiya. Hope HW going well. Don't forget - leftovers - microwave - use a plate! And sleep well."

"I guess she *is* trying to be a good Mum," Clara thought, "but sometimes she just seems ... unfair."

FOUR

A southerly had come through during the night. Clara hurried down the hill toward the Sailing Club. She could clearly see frothy lumps of foam scattered along the shore.

It was Wednesday. The Clubhouse looked closed, but the shed was open. Someone was around. Time to meet Crusty. Time to listen to more of his hints - advice - on *going fast*. The race on Saturday had been a disaster and despite having Crusty's words running through her head, *Wizz Kid* had come last. Billy had won again, making losing even harder to bear.

As she crossed the rigging lawn towards the *Creaky Shed*, Crusty rose up out of his dinghy and scrambled onto the jetty. He limped across the grass towards her. Clearly, he had been waiting for her.

"Poor result on Saturday," he mumbled. "Didn't listen to one thing I said, did ya."

In a rare moment of weakness, a tear welled up in the corner of Clara's eye. She had tried so hard. Crusty's words had been running around and around in her head all week, but she had failed yet again.

"OK kid, toughen up. Life is tough. Now back to basics. I watched your race and you made foolish mistakes, but the way in which you moved with *Wizz Kid* was clearly better."

"But I came last, Billy won again and I so want to beat him."

Crusty took a deep breath and looked out across the river; a stare that went further than the eye could see.

"Relax kid, I watched. Billy made a number of fundamental mistakes. You CAN beat him. Just work on one thing at a time. Now rig your boat and get on the water as quick as you can."

With that, he shuffled off to the jetty and waited for her to launch.

Soon she was cutting across the water, hanging out with all her might to counter the wind that clearly wanted to topple the boat.

Crusty rowed his dinghy out onto the river and called out to her as she passed, "Sail a big circle around my dinghy."

And then he yelled, with just a touch of excitement, "Work with the wind. Not against it."

Rowing his dinghy to keep it in position against the strong southerly, Crusty watched as Clara sailed around and around and around him. He said nothing. Just watched and rowed and watched.

Finally, he called, "OK, now the other way around."

Around and around Clara went. She was aware that he was watching every move she made. How she responded to the gusts. How she steered the boat. Adding up her strengths and weaknesses. Formulating a plan.

Abruptly, Crusty turned his dinghy toward *Wave Leaper.*

Calling out, "Good. See you next week," he was gone.

With that, Clara sailed to the slipway and began to pack up. As she looked across to where Crusty was, she could see him on board *Wave Leaper,* his dinghy bobbing patiently near her stern.

"That was a bit pointless," Clara moaned as she carried her mast into the shed. Again, no helpful advice from Crusty, she thought, but then he never really says much anyway. Admittedly, though, it was really good sailing. She felt satisfied. She even felt that *Wizz Kid* had enjoyed the strong wind.

Picking up her bag and pulling the shed's roller door down, she looked at her mobile and groaned.

"Late!" she mumbled to herself.

Every one of Clara's freckles was glowing from the brisk one kilometre jog, mainly uphill, back to home. Clara fought the gate, and was inside her home well before Mum arrived. She took a deep breath and readied herself to continue the lie about netball practice.

A few minutes later Mum all but blew into the house.

Like a southerly buster, she roared, "What's this I hear! Sailing on the river on a Wednesday with an old man. Not netball! You lied to me, you little river rat."

Without taking a breath, Mum shook her fists and continued to yell, "Explain yourself! And don't bother to lie. Mrs Jalna told me! You *know* she lives near that Banjo Point Sailing Club. She saw you out on the Gremlin with some old man paddling around you. She carried on about how good it was to see you listening and working so hard. As if I *knew* you were doing this! Whaaatt is going on! Well? Explain!"

Clara looked down at the gaps in the floorboards.

"Damn," she muttered. For the second time that day, her vision blurred as tears slipped from the corner of her eye.

Then the tension, created by her Mum's lack of support, turned to anger. Clara took a stance. She was ready to fight back.

Leaning into the words that tumbled out, she snapped, "You don't care! Other kids have their parents to help. I don't. You! Don't! Care!"

"Stop yourself right there, young lady. I work hard every day to keep you clothed and fed. And to let you sail! But it has become an obsession with you to the point of lying about netball. I don't accept that."

"At least at the Sailing Club I feel some people care. I feel a part of the community and I like it there."

"Answer me this", shouted Clara's Mum, "Who is that old man you are hanging out with? Don't you know how careful you need to be around creepy old men?"

"He's not creepy," Clara shouted, her top lip quivering. "A few weeks ago, I swam out in a strong westerly gale. Saved him AND his boat from the rocks while everybody else just watched. He offered to help me sail faster. A gift. His thanks. I need *his* help like he needed *mine*."

Clara's Mum, still furious, was breathing hard, her face an explosion of anger. Eventually, her rage crumbled.

She collapsed into the nearest chair, sighing, "I hope you are right, Clara".

Clara headed for her room, shouting over her shoulder, "I AM right! I am going to keep sailing. I am going to get good. I am going to beat Billy. You *cannot* stop me."

FIVE

The starting hooter blared and the Gremlins hopped off the start line, heading up the course towards the top mark. Southerly gusts pumped across the river. Clara hung over the side, confidently balancing *Wizz Kid*. A good start.

Clara was in a strong position, slightly ahead and to the windward side of Billy. She tacked. He tacked. Another wind shift, she tacked again. Once more, Billy followed. Fighting their way up the course, Clara was determined to stay ahead as long as she could.

Eventually, Billy got the bow of his boat ahead during a lull and, from that point on, he lead. Clara was excited. She had challenged him. That was good enough - for the moment.

Back at the Sailing Club, Clara de-rigged and slid *Wizz Kid* into the shed before heading into the Clubhouse. The Gremlin sailors were in their usual corner, clustered around their favourite table, chatting away about the race and the wind.

Tentatively, Clara approached. Instead of the usual cold shoulder from the group, Lindy moved a chair aside and invited Clara to take a seat.

"Well done for the first beat. You held Billy most of the way," Lindy grinned, eyes fixed on Clara.

"Thanks." Clara could feel her freckles reddening, a self-conscious response to the compliment.

Billy sat on the far side, smug in the knowledge that he had won again. But the challenge was there. He was very sure of that!

"How come you went so well today?" Lindy asked, "*Wizz Kidd* was fast in its day so we've been told, but that was a long time ago."

"I'm not sure," Clara lied, "The boat just felt light and I was lucky I guess."

Clara couldn't admit that she had a coach - Crusty, no less. She knew the truth would come out eventually. Her Mum certainly knew, as did her Mum's friend. The important thing was her growing confidence in Crusty as her coach. His approach was already making a difference.

*

Wednesday afternoon came around quickly, and with it a light wind. Clara was unsure whether to rig at all. Crossing the lawn, she saw Crusty walking across from the jetty; a lightness in his limping gait.

"Well done," he blurted, "that was fantastic last Saturday. I knew you could do it."

He was so animated that his long grey pigtail flicked from side to side as he spoke. She had never seen him so happy - so excited! It was clear that he had worked at preparing for this moment. Clara couldn't help but grin.

"You kept ahead almost all the way to the top mark. You were fantastic and it looks like old *Wizz Kid* is at last coming alive again. She was a very fast boat when I sailed her last."

Clara stood still. She stared at Crusty.

And then, in one breath, she burst out, "Crusty! Are. You. John. Brenton!"

He didn't seem to hear her. He continued to twitter on about the race and the wind and how Clara had been hanging out over the side and that *Wizz Kid* was fast again - at last.

Then he stopped. Turning to Clara, he looked at her as if she had just appeared.

"What was that, *yungun'*?"

Clara turned toward Crusty and gently asked, "Are you *the* John Brenton who won the Gremlin Championship in '65?"

"Mmm," he replied, as a faraway look clouded out the present. "Gremlins were pretty new in the scheme of things. My dad built *Wizz Kid* for me when I was around your age. In her day, she was the fastest Gremlin in this country. Was hoping all these years that someone would come along and sail her as she deserves."

Suddenly he was animated again, "Now, let's get on the water. Hurry. We need to work to win."

Clara rigged up with haste, but this time Crusty stayed to help. His hands were claw-like. Still, he could quickly do up shackles and tie knots. Working together, the boat was soon ready to launch, but Crusty began talking about sail settings. It was as if he was a wound-up rubber band.

As a coach, he proved to be excellent, explaining what needed to be done, why the settings needed to be this way or that and then asking Clara to explain it all back to him.

Clara's head was overflowing - so many settings, so many options, and so many reasons why. Now to remember it all!

Suddenly, it was as if Crusty had exposed his soul. He went quiet, looked into the distance. Then he stopped, looked at *Wizz Kid,* rigged and ready to sail, and turned toward the jetty.

Glancing back at Clara, he nodded his head and pointed his finger, "Remember what's important. *Especially* remember to feel the wind on the sails, feel when it's powerful and feel when it's slow. I'll watch you on Saturday. Good luck, *yungun'.*"

And with that, he was gone.

Clara quickly de-rigged her Gremlin, stepped out of her faded wetsuit, grabbed her bag and headed home.

She knew she was late again. She liked to be home before her Mum, settled into her homework, keeping to routine, despite her Wednesday training sessions.

"Damn!"

The front door was unlocked. Mum was home. Hopefully in a good mood.

"Hello, Sweetie," Mum called from the kitchen. "I phoned the Sailing Club."

She twisted around as Clara entered the kitchen.

"I wanted to find out who this old guy was," she said with a smile, "and who else was around when you were down there and if it was safe."

Clara felt her mood lighten. Mum had actually done something for *her.*

"I spoke to a man who said he was the Commodore. What does that mean?"

Clara's heart sank.

Mum went on, oblivious to the mess she may have created.

"He said it was quite safe and 'Crusty' - that's the name he gave me - was a harmless old Vietnam Veteran who hated everybody and everything. He lives on a boat in front of the Sailing Club. Oh - and the old guys at the Sailing Club were already watching out for you."

Clara took a few deep breaths. She was angry. She could feel her face reddening. She realised that her Mum had tried to do the right thing but that she had no idea of the potential havoc she may have caused.

Tears threatened to spill from Clara's eyes.

Wiping her hand across her face, Clara began, her voice tight and controlled, "Mum, the Commodore is Billy's granddad - his Pop. Billy is basically my arch enemy. He's the arrogant kid who always wins. The last thing I want is for that... that... one person, who humiliates me at school all the time, to find out that I am training with Crusty. Billy hates Crusty. This was supposed to be my secret. Now you've told... you've told... everybody!"

As she stood in the doorway facing her Mum, the tears flowed down her cheeks.

Mum drew Clara toward her, wrapping her arms around her daughter, "I'm sorry, Sweetie. I thought I was helping and I wanted you to be safe. I'm sorry."

Clara's mind whirled in confusion. Was Mum now on her side? Was Mum now supporting her ambition to be good at sailing? Clara was happy that Mum was supportive, but she probably sunk Clara's plan in her first attempt to help.

Snuggled into her Mum's shoulder, Clara mumbled, "I don't know what to do now. What if Billy gets some coaching? I was just starting to challenge him. I was ahead of him for a long way on Saturday," she sniffled, and with this thought, a smirk formed in the corner of her mouth.

Mum lifted Clara's chin and looked gently into her eyes, "That's fantastic. Tell me what happened."

She moved Clara to a chair at the dining room table while Clara recounted moment by moment the race on Saturday - how she had started and kept ahead for so long. When she finally finished, Mum was smiling - a proud smile that Clara could not remember ever seeing on her Mum's face.

"Wow, Clara," she beamed, "I can see you are really enjoying this and it
sounds like you are pretty good at it."

As an afterthought, she added, "Don't rush home next Wednesday afternoon. I'm confident that you are safe - the summer days are getting longer. Take advantage of every moment."

Clara winked, "Thanks, Mum, I would love that."

SIX

Crusty hobbled across the rigging lawn as Clara opened up the roller door of the *Creaky Shed*. She knew that something was wrong. Crusty was different. His attitude had changed and he was in a hurry and impatient.

Without even a g'day, he muttered, "Come on, *yungun'*. Let's get this boat on the water. The pressure is on."

"Ok Crusty... by the way, Mum is happy for me to stay later this afternoon. I just need to get home before dark."

"Excellent," he scowled.

"What's happened, Crusty? I thought we were going well."

Crusty was staring across the river, seemingly lost in some other world. Clara waited. She now knew he'd come back in a minute.

Suddenly, he turned towards her, his grey pigtail following seconds later, growling, "Billy was down practising yesterday. He had Mike Ayers training him. Ayers doesn't just offer to train any kid. This is getting serious. There is a lot on the line now."

Clara's heart sank. She knew that it was her Mum who had let the cat out of the bag. She knew Crusty knew. And now Crusty was going to take it out on her.

"Crusty... please... Mum phoned the Sailing Club to ask if I was safe here on Wednesdays," Clara blurted out. "A lady she knows told my Mum I was doing extra sailing with someone. Mum spoke to Billy's Pop. It was not me. I'm so sorry. I really am. I really tried not to let anyone else know."

Crusty turned towards Clara and for a moment he stared at her, as if startled. His gaze softened. A light punch on her shoulder, he moved toward the rigging.

"OK kid, let's get you on the water and get you *feeling* what fast is. No argument - we are training to win!"

His voice rose, "Let's get rigged. We have work to do."

The afternoon was a blur of tacks and gybes as Crusty encouraged Clara to *feel* the boat - to *be* the boat.

"Roll the boat when you tack. Go again. This time make it slower in the beginning and come out of the turn more quickly."

He continued, firing more tactics at Clara as she threw herself into her training.

"Fully extend your legs as you hang over the side. Good! Now bob your weight over each little wave. C'mon, push the *Wizz* forward with each wave."

As she followed Crusty's directions, Clara was loving each movement - each skill - despite the effort of keeping herself balanced.

"Good, keep that up. Drive the boat forward with your body."

And then, as if preaching to the breeze, he called out, "Feel the wind. Be the boat."

Back on shore, Clara tumbled onto the lawn. She was sore all over; her legs were tired and her tummy muscles ached. She rose with a satisfied sigh and began packing *Wizz Kid* away. She watched Crusty hobbling towards her from where he had tied up his dinghy.

Looking Clara straight in the eye, he explained, "I don't want to complicate your life with old feuds, but I would like to help you to sail to the best of your ability and beat Billy in the upcoming Gremlin National Titles at Henry's Bay. Had some very good races there myself, back in the day.

With that, he turned and headed off.

After a few paces, he stopped and looked back over his shoulder, throwing out an unexpected comment, "Maybe you are ready for a new sail?" and then to finish off, he instructed, "On Saturday, make sure you enjoy the sailing. Sail your *own* race and ignore Billy and all the rest of the kids on the race course. *Yungun'*, the most important thing is to have fun."

And then, nearing the jetty, he hollered, "Holidays start soon, kid, more time for more training!"

The walk up the hill from the Clubhouse seemed steeper than it had ever been as Clara, muscles aching from the hard training, mused over the day's strategies, aware of the steep learning curve she had experienced. Gasping for breath as she rounded the top of the hill, Clara leaned against a very old, and very solid, gum tree. She remembered Crusty's rather odd comment about a new sail.

"What did Crusty mean - a new sail? And where would that come from?" she thought.

*

Dragging her bag into the lounge room, Clara flopped into the closest chair. Mum surveyed the muddle of red hair, and the crumple of clothes that was her exhausted daughter - a rag doll slumped into an armchair. Beneath that mop of curly hair, and despite her fatigue, Clara looked up - bright eyes shining with enthusiasm.

"Crusty was different today. He was grumpy, but happy at the same time. I think he is enjoying the training, but I think there is something else going on. He wants me sign up to the Gremlin Nationals in December... at Henry's Bay Sailing Club. He says it is really cool down there and the kids are talking about sailing the eight nautical mile trip down to Henry's Bay the week before. Oh Mum... an adventure - a real adventure. Mum... a National Titles with prizes and.... and... medals. Awards for the top result, plus top boy, top girl! And then there are prizes for the Sailing Club that performs the best. An Under Sixteen Regatta for only Gremlin sailors! There will be Gremlins, Mum, from all over the country. Whatcha think? Please, Mum, say yes!"

And before Mum could respond, Clara blurted out, "He thinks I need a new sail if I want to win!"

"Well, hold on now," Clara's Mum frowned, "not that that's going to happen in this lifetime. How much is a Gremlin sail anyway?"

Clara had no idea but she promised to find out, knowing that there would be a limited chance of ever being able to buy a new one.

SEVEN

Setting up for the Saturday race, Clara pulled *Wizz Kid* out of the old *Creaky Shed*. Distracted by the sailing strategies storming around in her head, she returned from collecting her mast, and suddenly stopped. Her friend - her *Wizz Kid* - was shiny. It had been transformed. The paint work gleamed. Even the rust marks, where the chainplates were attached to hold up the mast, were gone. She carefully put the mast down beside the renovated boat. Taking a slow circuit around *Wizz Kid,* she was astounded by the subtle, and not so subtle, changes in the *Wizz*. She knew, without doubt, that this was Crusty's work. Her surprise turned to a sense of pride as she admired *her* Gremlin glistening in the sunshine.

Lindy approached from the Clubhouse, stood beside Clara, and grinned, taking in *Wizz Kid's* restored appearance.

"Wow! Looks like new!" she smiled, and then placing her hand on Clara's shoulder, faced her and calmly stated, "I hope you stay ahead of Billy today."

Clara beamed from ear to ear. She knew the other kids' dads were often down at the Sailing Club, fiddling with their kids' boats; maintaining them, polishing them. As *Wizz Kid* was a Banjo Point Sailing Club boat, no effort was made to maintain her since she was donated many decades ago.

Clara rigged, and scampered back to the Clubhouse for the pre-race briefing. Returning to the rigging lawn, she wheeled *Wizz Kid* across to the slipway. She hesitated, worried that the brightly polished hull would get scratched if she pulled it up onto the slipway while putting the dolly back onto the rigging lawn.

A dilemma for Clara - other kids always had some help. With extreme care, she slipped the dolly, with her boat nestled on it, into the water. The dolly slipped just below the surface as the boat floated free. A firm hand reached across to steady the dolly

"I'll get this for you, Clara. Wouldn't want to scratch that fancy hull now, would we?"

It was Billy's Pop. Clara was so taken aback that she only just managed to blurt out an embarrassed, "Thanks."

The overall race results were similar to previous weeks. Billy won again! However, the margin between Billy's performance and Clara's was definitely less. It was evident to all that the newly renovated *Wizz Kid* was making a comeback. Maybe the rumours were true - perhaps *Wizz Kid* was a *fast* boat.

*

Wednesday afternoon. A light breeze whispered around the water and across Banjo Point. A hint of clouds was building in the western sky. Clara pulled *Wizz Kid* - her beautiful jewel - out of the shed. Readying the mast for insertion, she rubbed her eyes in disbelief. The mast had been renovated, and buffed. Shiny new rivets had replaced the old corroded ones. The *Wizz* was sparkling.

Even Crusty seemed 'renovated'. He moved differently - a spring in his step, if that was possible. Clearly the challenge of getting his old boat up to speed had invigorated him. He bubbled with enthusiasm as he helped Clara rig.

"Today is 'start practice'. There will always be other boats in your way - you need to have some practice on what to do when this happens. You know *starts* are critical, so I'm going to be just another boat on the start line for you to avoid."

Crusty threw a couple of plastic milk bottles into the river. They were about five metres apart and held in place by a piece of string with a weight attached that sank, obediently, to the bottom of the river. A nifty start line on which to practice.

"OK, I need you to start on port. When it's one minute to go, I'll call out, 'one minute'. Get your timing right. It's up to you from then on."

With the light breeze swirling around, she counted down the seconds for the first start. And then, in disbelief, she saw Crusty rowing his dinghy straight towards *Wizz Kid*.

"Get out of the way," Clara called.

Crusty looked back at her, almost grinning. Crying out 'starboard', he steered his dinghy directly into her path. Clara glared at him as she missed the end of the line. She spun the boat around and tried again.

"Aha!" challenged Crusty, "Try that again."

Clara did, again and again, as Crusty continued to get in her way, testing her reactions and adeptness at moving her boat this way and that way to avoid his dinghy.

"OK, swap around. You start on starboard now."

As he rowed and rowed, dark patches of sweat began to emerge across Crusty's old t-shirt.

"Damn," he puffed, as Clara slipped past him, "I should have used an outboard motor for this."

Clara approached the line, wind to starboard. This changed the plan. Crusty had to get out of *her* way now. But instead of moving out of her way, he rowed straight into her path!

"Starboard," Clara screamed, but Crusty did his best to get in her way. Narrowly slipping past Crusty, Clara missed the end of the line.

"That's not fair, Crusty. You can't do that!"

"But I just did. Get over it. Try again."

The game continued into the late afternoon. Clara tried again and again as Crusty did his best to mess up her start.

"Enough," wheezed Crusty, "I can't keep this up. Time to pack it in. Do a few circles so I can get your dolly ready. Don't want to scratch that shiny hull."

And with that, Clara thought she saw him smile; the sort that comes from sharing a secret.

As Clara busied herself with the packing up, she was surprised to see Gary, one of the older Sailing Club members, wander over to talk with Crusty. He appeared a bit younger than Crusty, less tanned, had no tattoos and spoke like a *fancy pants,* or so Clara felt.

Intrigued, Clara stood quietly, observing this seemingly rare act. She had not seen Crusty talk to anybody in all the time she had known him. It was further surprising when, listening to their conversation, she learned that, together, they had worked on *Wizz Kid*'s mast over the past couple of days.

As she picked up her bag to go, Gary smiled, "Good luck on Saturday. You are beginning to sail really well."

"Thanks. I promise to do my best."

"Good. We'd like to see *Wizz Kid* win. She was the fastest Gremlin in our Sailing Club for quite a few years. A lot of people here have sailed her at some time or another over the years," Gary added.

Clara headed home with her head in a whirl. She was getting so much help. So much effort had been put into *Wizz Kid* recently, but it all added up to more pressure.

A tiny dark cloud of doubt added to her nervousness as she thought ahead to Saturday - the race that she was now expected to win.

EIGHT

By Thursday evening, Clara was as 'sick as a dog'. An aching head, her nose was running and her throat was raging. Mum had her issues, especially in relation to being organised, but she certainly could make a patient feel that there was hope.

"You'll be right tomorrow," and, tucking Clara into bed, she dosed Clara with a 'flu tablet and cough syrup, leaving cough drops on Clara's bedside table. Although Clara slept deeply, she woke in pain the next morning; her body aching all over.

"No school today," Mum said cheerily.

All day Friday, and into the evening, Clara was dosed up again and again. With hands on hips, Mum teased her, warning that if Clara had not improved by morning, she was going to find her a comfortable place to die - just leave her there to get on with it.

Saturday morning dawned. Clara woke feeling more energetic, despite her wheezing and the occasional sneeze. She refrained from suggesting that she was able to sail, knowing that Mum would shut that idea down in an instant.

Instead, she wrapped up warmly in her favourite hoody and headed for the Sailing Club. A strong and gusty southerly was building. Boats were capsizing at the start line, and rescue boats were kept busy returning bedraggled sailors and their water-logged boats to the rigging lawn.

From the upper deck of the Clubhouse, Clara could see the race course. It was a difficult afternoon to be racing and she was feeling thankful that she wasn't on the water. However, disappointment played across her face. The strong winds meant that the Gremlins were going fast - and fast was fun. She desperately wanted to test herself in a strong wind.

But today was not the day!

Only three boats finished and, for once, Billy did not win. He had capsized twice, managing to recover, but he was not a happy boy when he arrived back at the rigging lawn. With his dad busy on a rescue boat, there was no one to help him retrieve his boat, nor to help him de-rig. The final straw for Billy was a sardonic grin from Matt, a former Gremlin sailor, who quipped, "Toughen up, Princess!."

"Bugger off, you puffed up fart," Billy shrieked back, and stormed off to the change room, leaving his boat with the mast up; the sail blowing over the side in the wind.

Before dragging her still unwell body up the hill, Clara decided to check on *Wizz Kid*. She was there, in the *Creaky Shed*, waiting patiently for her. Oddly, Clara felt sad that she had seemingly let *Wizz Kid* down. Silently, she promised to make it up. Turning to leave, she noticed an envelope in her rope bag. Another note from Crusty, she thought. She quickly stuffed it deep into her hoody's pocket and left.

Quietly slipping into the house, Clara moved to her bedroom and shut her door. Pulling out the letter, she studied the envelope - white with one of those little windows. A used - no - a recycled envelope. She plucked out a tiny piece of paper, one that had been folded over too many times as if it contained a deep secret.

When Clara finally got the now crumpled paper open, it revealed a scrawled note. It read:

"Crusty is dangerous. He killed people in the Vietnam War.
Be careful, little girl."

Clara placed the note on her desk and, as if the note was dirty, wiped her hands on her jeans.

Her mind spun. What was this about? And then from deep down, tears welled, blurring her vision. She was crying. Deep slow sobs that just kept coming. Curling onto her bed, she buried her face deep into her pillow.

The one person in her life who had taken a real interest in her, the person who appeared to be stable, who encouraged her and focussed on her strengths as a sailor, was suddenly being presented as an evil monster. Life was so unfair. So very unfair. And it seemed to be mostly unfair to her.

Mum softly knocked on the door.

"Are you OK, Sweetie?" she called from the landing.

Gently opening the door, she saw Clara lying on the bed with her pillow over her head. Mum quietly settled next to Clara and gently rubbed her back. As she tried to soothe her daughter, she saw the crumpled paper and read its message.

"What's this?" Mum exploded, "Who wrote this? Where did you get this?"

Suddenly Mum was animated. "Speak to me, girl. Where did this come from?"

Clara wrapped the pillow even more tightly around her ears, sobbing uncontrollably.

Mum stormed from Clara's room and in seconds was on the phone. She could hear her Mum talking quietly to someone and then ... her Mum's anger erupted.

"Not Billy's Pop. Please, not Billy's Pop," Clara held her breath, pleading in silence.

Mum raised her voice and Clara knew who her Mum had rung. It *was* Billy's Pop, the Commodore of the Banjo Point Sailing Club; the one place in which she had begun to feel accepted and valued.

Shaking and tearful, Clara's feeling of hope was suffocated by this note - filled with malice. Everything had collapsed. Everything.

She was aware that Mum was back, sitting beside her on the bed. Trying to console Clara, Mum continued to rub Clara's back, massaging across her shoulders and neck.

Leaning close to Clara, she whispered, "Sweetie, listen. There is more to this than we know. There is a bigger picture and you have landed in the middle of a much bigger story. Clean yourself up. We are going down to the Sailing Club. We will talk with Billy's Pop and try to get to the bottom of all this."

Clara raised her head from her pillow. Releasing one long deep rolling sob, she looked at her Mum who looked back at her. Today, they were a team.

"I know how much this means to you and I need to get to the bottom of it for you, Clara."

Dragging herself from her bed, Clara blew her nose, wiped her face, and turned towards her Mum. Grabbing her hand, they walked down the stairs and out through the difficult gate, towards the hill leading down to the Sailing Club.

NINE

The Race Office at the Clubhouse was up a steep staircase. Clara's Mum was already uncomfortable from the brisk walk toward the Sailing Club, only to be faced with steep ladder-like steps up to the Commodore's Office. Focussed on the conversation to come, they climbed the stairs, knowing that this really was the better place to talk. It was private.

Billy's Pop ushered them in and offered them faded pink plastic chairs. He was calm. His presence was warm and inviting. Although it was Clara's Mum's first visit to the Banjo Point Sailing Club, he made her feel welcome.

"Crusty grew up around the Club and sailed *Wizz Kid* when he was your age, Clara," he started. "A few years later, he was drafted into the army during the Vietnam War and served a number of tours of duty. He was injured in the Battle of Long Tan, which is why he limps."

"That's what his tattoo says," piped up Clara.

"Yes, that's it, but the real story begins when the lads came back from the war. There were people in our Sailing Club who said that the lads shouldn't have gone, let alone do a second and a third tour of duty! It was a difficult time. Some people left because of the unpleasantness that it caused. Crusty took it all very badly and I don't think he has been back inside the actual Clubhouse for fifty years or more."

"He went away to work on big ships and returned to this area when he retired. He bought *Wave Leaper* to sail the world. As you know, that nearly ended on the rocks just down from our Sailing Club if it had not been for you, young lady."

He shifted in his chair and folded his hands together.

Turning toward Clara, he continued, his eyes gently focussed on her, "There are still people in this Sailing Club who call him a 'baby killer' and the wounds of that feud are still very raw for some people. I presume that the note came from one of those people. Crusty, despite his lonely ways, is a good guy caught in a bad bit of history that he can't forget. There are those who keep trying to make it worse."

"Why are they picking on *me* then," Clara blurted out. "I have nothing against them."

"Well, that's the point. You, Clara, have been a wonderful addition to our Sailing Club. You sail with an instinct that is incredible for your age but, more importantly, you have brought Crusty to life. You have given him a focus - an incentive. You are the daughter he never had and - well the chance to help you learn to sail is the best thing in his life."

There was a pause as the big sliding door rolled across the end of the Clubhouse below and crashed to a halt.

"Clara, please don't give up. Banjo Point Sailing Club needs your talents and I think you are happy here. Is that right?"

"I am loving it here. It's like a second home to me. I could not imagine life without sailing, and now, even more so."

*

While Mum huffed up the hill, Clara skipped around her saying, "I told you it was a good place, Mum. I told you."

Mum grunted a reply, then stopped to catch her breath. Gazing back down the hill, the Sailing Club, the river and the moored boats dotted along the shore, created a peaceful landscape.

"Not a bad bunch, I'd say. So, which is Crusty's boat?"

"Over there, Mum," Clara pointed. "The cream-coloured boat with two masts."

Wave Leaper bobbed patiently at her mooring, her dinghy swinging out the back. A figure was busy on the foredeck with a paint tin and a brush.

"Is that Crusty on board?" Mum asked. "Looks like an old bloke with a grey pigtail from here."

"Yep, that's him. Rumour is that he plans to sail *Wave Leaper* right around the world - solo - as soon as she's ready."

TEN

With only a week left of the school year, Clara's homework was non-existent. The wind was perfect for training and so she arranged to sail with Lindy on Tuesday afternoon. Crusty would be training Clara on Wednesday so the time with Lindy would be free from the intensity that Crusty brought to their recent sessions.

Clara appreciated Lindy's company. They would be on their own; just the two of them enjoying the wind, the water, and their friendship. Lindy and Clara were excited as they skipped down the hill together.

As the girls crossed the rigging lawn towards the shed, they noticed something that they had never seen around the Sailing Club before - a big RIB with a centre console alongside the launching ramp.

The roller door to the shed was already open and pulling his boat out backwards was Billy, followed by a fit looking elderly man who was carrying Billy's mast.

Billy begrudgingly uttered a 'hi' while the old guy merely waved a 'hello girls'.

Both girls looked at each other for a moment.

Lindy shrugged, "He being here is not going to stop us. Let's get going."

Soon their boats were out and masts up, readying to launch, when the old guy came over.

"I'm about to coach Billy this afternoon on 'starts' and strategies for getting off the line quickly. It would be good if you could join in to make up the numbers. I'm sure you will also learn something, 'though I *will* be focussed on Billy."

The girls looked at each other, hesitated, and then Clara asked, "What do you think Lindy? It should be OK?"

Lindy gave Clara a long look. They both knew that helping Billy was a bad strategy. Yet having a bit of coaching would be good.

The girls' hesitation nudged the coach into saying, "Sorry, I'm Mark Ayers. I normally coach the Australian Petrel Team, but they are having a couple of days off before we head to Florida for the World Titles. Billy's Pop and I go back a long way when we sailed here in the '60s."

Lindy came to life, eyes opened wide in surprise.

"Ahhh, I've heard of you. You coached the Australian Olympic team once."

Ayers grinned and nodded in reply.

*

In no time, the three sailors, on board their Gremlins, were counting down the seconds for each 'race' start. Mark called out instructions to Billy. The girls worked hard to hear all of his explanations and tips - an unexpected lesson of which they were quietly thankful.

When the coaching session was over, and Billy, Lindy and Clara were packing up on the lawn, Mark approached Clara, "You did really well today. You sail without seeming to think about it. You make the wind your friend. More importantly, you move as if you and the boat are one."

Clara grinned. Her heart warmed, remembering that Mark's words were almost exactly Crusty's first lesson.

Clara wondered if Crusty would take her sailing with Billy and Mark Ayers as an insult, or would he encourage her to just benefit from the experience, she hoped he would not take it badly.

ELEVEN

Wednesday afternoon. Training time. Dark patches reflected on the water from gusty squalls as they scurried across the sky towards the coast. Rain was evident. Clara knew that Crusty expected her to sail - rain or shine. Grabbing her rain jacket, she headed towards Banjo Point Sailing Club.

Dragging *Wizz Kid* out of the shed, Clara busied herself rigging up, readying herself for a windy and wet afternoon. Once the sail was up, it was clear that *Wizz Kid* did not want to sit still. As she was readying herself in the *Creaky Shed*, heavy gusts of winds would send Clara dashing out to hold *Wizz Kid* down.

Zipping up her old wetsuit, she was finally ready. Despite the stress, she knew well that the conditions for training were excellent. The challenge, including the thrill of sailing fast, excited Clara.

She waited. She gazed toward *Wave Leaper*. She waited. It was eerily quiet despite the howl of the wind. Crusty did not appear. Maybe he had seen her sailing with Billy and Marks Ayers the day before? Maybe he thought she had betrayed his trust, maybe she had disappointed him.

She worried. Maybe Crusty was sick? Or had something else happened?

She launched *Wizz Kid*, leaving the dolly in the water. In no time, she was skipping across the river towards *Wave Leaper.* Sailing around the stern, Clara hollered, "Crusty? Cruuusssty?"

As she came closer on a second pass, Crusty appeared in the companionway. His eyes were red.

Wiping his nose as he spoke, Crusty apologised, "Sorry, *yungun'*, I've caught that bug you had last week and I really should not put my head out any further than this."

Clara sailed back and forth in short tacks as Crusty hollered across to her, "Sail without me. Sail for the joy of it. Sail just for fun. Sail fast."

And with that he went below.

The river could be a lonely place when the weather was rough. Being the only boat on this part of the water made Clara a little nervous. She turned the boat southeast and beat into the wind; the crests of the waves breaking into white horses as she sailed onto them. *Wizz Kid* was alive. The power of the wind had Clara hanging over the side with all her might. Spray curled over the bow and blew away downwind as she burst through each wave.

In no time, she had moved far from the shoreline, heading to where the gusts were stronger. As the wind whipped in from the Great Southern Ocean, Clara was rolling her body back and forth with each swell, feeling *Wizz Kid's* power over the waves. For Clara, this was hard work. Despite her tummy muscles aching from the effort of keeping *Wizz Kid* on course, she was having fun. *Wizz Kid* was moving fast.

In a lull between gusts, Clara looked back towards the Clubhouse. With a chill, she realised how far she had sailed. She was totally alone. Not one other craft was on the river at this moment. Tacking the Gremlin around, and with the wind behind her, she hung over the very back corner of the boat, balancing her weight against the wind. *Wizz Kid* took off and planed at top speed down the face of the waves. Reaching the trough, Clara turned slightly towards the wind. The wave caught up and she was off once more, a shower of spray moving across the bow

She was the wind, she was *Wizz Kid,* and she was loving every moment. But regardless of the fun, she knew she was not heading towards the Clubhouse. She knew that she would need to gybe the boat around onto the other tack - soon.

"I can do this," Clara affirmed, more to give herself courage than anything else. She timed the manoeuvre, finding a trough between the waves. Grabbing the boom, she yanked it across the boat. Diving across to the other side, *Wizz Kid* sped up again, skidding down the faces of the waves in showers of spray.

Clara, bravely and determinedly, repeated this action. She knew that she could handle it. She had *Wizz Kid* in perfect balance with the waves, the wind - and, yes, herself. She was in control. Sailing her Gremlin.

"I'm not afraid of this," she shouted to no-one. "I'm a real sailor. The wind *is* my friend."

As the saying goes '*pride goeth before the fall*'. Clara's words had barely been uttered when, to her horror, she noticed the leeward stay had lost its pin. The stay, itself, was no longer attached. She knew that the mast would remain up as long as she kept on the tack, but that meant heading straight toward the black rocks on the river bank - the rocks where *Wave Leaper* had nearly floundered a few months ago. Gybing was an option but she also knew that gybing would mean that the mast would tumble over the side, ending up in the rolling waves.

Clara screamed in fear.

Rising panic clouded her thoughts. Calling for help was pointless with only the raging river and the white crests to hear her. She needed to think *FAST*. Her mind raced through the options. If she went onto the black rocks, she risked smashing the boat. Hurting herself. Gybing and dropping the rig was her only option. A scary option.

She gybed and the rig - mast, boom, stays, sheets and lines - toppled into the water.

Clara had to get this mess - ropes and sheets and lines and spars - onboard as quickly as possible. *Wizz Kid* rocked gently with the mast in the water. Clara stumbled around, trying to pull the rig back on board. Balancing herself, and, with a massive effort, she pulled the tangled mess of rigging back on board.

With the mast tied and held in position along the length of the boat, she held up a corner of the sail to catch the wind. *Wizz Kid* responded and together they slowly headed back towards the Sailing Club.

*

As Clara approached the slipway, pulling up the rudder and centreboard at the last minute, she jumped out to steady the boat. And there was Crusty. Holding her dolly. Ready to help *Wizz Kid* back onto land.

Crusty was animated. His blue eyes bright; his grey pigtail swishing around like a whip as he excitedly helped Clara get back onto land. Once de-rigged, Crusty lowered himself onto the lawn, coughing and coughing, battling to breathe.

Crusty, clearing his throat, smiled at Clara, saying, "Hey, fine effort. Good recovery but... mmm... what happened, *yungun*?"

Looking at *Wizz Kid*, he waited for Clara to explain.

"It was fun," she paused, "and... uh... scary... really scary. But it was fast, Crusty... fast. The pin came out of the chain plate and I just knew it would end badly. But here I am... with *Wizz Kid*."

Crusty tried to clear his throat, coughed again, sneezed twice and then managed to wheeze out, "Well done, Clara. I'm gonna tell ya now. You are an excellent sailor. I'm proud of ya," and with that he coughed again, rose carefully, and shuffled off to his dinghy.

Clara watched him, thinking how much older - and fragile - he looked today.

Walking up that hill towards home was always thinking time. As Clara chewed over the events of the afternoon, her head spun with the thrill of the moment, the feeling of fear, and the excitement. She felt proud of her outing. It was tough sailing. And then a rigging disaster. Followed by a good recovery.

Crusty had called her Clara, not '*yungun*', for the first time.

"Why was that?" she wondered.

"What if the wind had blown her *away* from Banjo Point Sailing Club, eastward towards Banjo Point Lighthouse... the ocean?" she thought.

A shiver of something akin to fear whipped over her as she realised the dire consequences that would have unfurled if she had been washed out to sea. Reprimanding herself with a 'better be a little more careful next time' comment, she turned the corner towards home.

TWELVE

Clara skipped down the hill. The Banjo Point Sailing Club seemed to be shimmering in the afternoon summer sun.

This was her last training session before the Nationals. Nervous, but excited, she knew Crusty would make this session special. She had learnt to *be the boat* - to *feel the boat*.

The wind felt perfect today.

Crusty was already on the rigging lawn. He had recovered from his cold, and, even from a distance, one could see that his energy had returned. He had dragged *Wizz Kid* from the *Creaky Shed*. She could see him fussing over the *Wizz*.

Clara crossed through the Clubhouse and out onto the rigging lawn. And then she stopped. Next to *Wizz Kid* was a green and red sail bag.

Her heart skipped a beat.

Crusty looked up, grinning rather mischievously.

"It's yours. A number of the old blokes in our Sailing Club passed the hat around," Crusty explained. "It's a gift to *Wizz Kid* - to you - in recognition of *your* attempts to make her famous again. Polished hull, refitted mast and now a new sail. Plus a skipper who always does her best. The old boat may well shine again."

Clara looked at the ground. She couldn't look Crusty in the eye.

"I don't know if I can - if it will," she whispered, "but I'll do my best Crusty. I feel scared. I may let you down."

"Enough of that talk. Let's pull up the new sail and see how it goes."

The new sail 'crackled' as they unrolled it. Clara smiled a deep long smile. She knew she was lucky - very lucky.

*

On the walk home after training, she was absorbed with her thoughts - the smell of the new sail, the sound of it, but, more importantly, how fast *Wizz Kid* responded as she tacked this way and that. There was nothing more important at that moment in time. The National Gremlin Titles was becoming a reality - a week to go.

Before she knew it, she was up the hill and home.

Stumbling in through the front door, Clara was already shouting excitedly, "Mum! Mum... Crusty and his mates bought *Wizz Kid* a new sail. *Wizz* flew this afternoon."

Mum, distractedly, proffered a smile, saying, "That's great, Sweetie. I hope it all goes well. Uh, just to let you know... I'm going out tonight... um... make sure you get to bed early."

And with that Mum re-focussed on what she had been doing, her back to Clara.

"Uh... OK, Mum."

Clara stared icily at her Mum's back for a moment, silently thinking 'thanks for being enthusiastic about the new sail' before skipping up the stairs to her room.

Registering for the Nationals had not been easy. Mum had grumbled about the entry fee, about her being away, camping over at Henry's Bay Sailing Club; even about having to pay to feed her.

Mum had grumbled about everything recently. Clara was starting to feel that Mum, once again, was not there for her.

Fortunately, Mum's negativity was overshadowed by the gift of the new sail in addition to Clara's recent excellent results in the Saturday Gremlin races. Crusty had been a great coach. She knew that Billy had a well-known coach but she believed in Crusty and remained positive - excited.

With her usual 'Bye, sleep well, and I'll see you in the morning' response and her usual *afterthought* of 'leftovers are in the 'fridge', Clara's Mum headed out the door. Clara peered through the window, watching her Mum walking towards the bus stop. Clara thought that her Mum seemed different - smaller than usual - as if the world was weighing her down.

The house groaned sometimes, but it seemed more obvious when Clara was alone. She huddled in front of the TV with her reheated dinner. Football and variety shows were boring. Even the movie looked too scary, so she made her way up the stairs to her bedroom.

Snuggling in under her duvet, she pulled open her set English novel for the upcoming Year 10, and settled into a night of reading. In no time, her eyelids grew heavy.

Slipping the book onto the side table, she clicked off the lamp, and stared into the darkness, imagining what tomorrow would be like.

THIRTEEN

Sails flapped as the boats lined up on the rigging lawn ready for the trip to Henry's Bay Sailing Club. Eight nautical miles they were reminded - a long way for these budding sailors.

They were nervous, but excited and enthused as they listened and responded to the clear instructions. Sailing together, as a group, was vital.

Many of the parents would follow in the Sailing Club's Committee Boat, fondly called *The Pearl*, with their kids' launching dollies. The Gremlins would be stored at Henry's Bay Sailing Club in anticipation of the Nationals the following Thursday - an event that would finish on Sunday - four days later.

If things could go wrong, it did!

The Pearl would not start.

The Gremlin team was long gone. The launching dollies remained on the rigging lawn, lined up. Ready to go. Parents milled around wondering what to do. Someone suggested placing the launching dollies on the roof of their cars, knowing they would need to drive the long way around to

Henry's Bay. They would certainly arrive well after their young sailors.

To add to the dilemma, they had to consider the team's safety. What if something happened to one or any of the young sailors during the crossing?

Crusty had *Wave Leaper* tied alongside the wharf. He had helped Clara rig, planning to sail south to Henry's Bay alone, he already had *Wizz Kid's* dolly on *Wave Leaper's* foredeck.

He was not prepared for what happened next.

Parents and grandparents began climbing onto *Wave Leaper,* tying their dollies onto the front deck, and passing their eskies across to each other. Within fifteen minutes, twenty or more people were onboard *Wave Leaper*.

"Pirates!" Crusty thought. There was little that he could do or say.

He had felt bullied. Without even asking him, he was forced to transport these *pirates* plus eight launching dollies.

He struggled through the endless thanks from the mums. He ignored the offers from the dads and granddads to help raise the sails as soon as they had rounded the headland.

It was just too much for Crusty. As the parents settled around the cockpit, he looked at no-one and appeared not to hear anybody.

Directing his gaze upon the horizon, he clasped the wheel with both hands and steered *Wave Leaper* south. The engine chugged, while the exhaust spluttered the cooling water out in puffs of steam.

*

Crusty stood stiffly at the wheel: rigid, unyielding. A statue amongst the relaxed crowd chilling in the stern of his boat. He felt surrounded by the enemy, shallow people whose families had stabbed him in the back on his return from Vietnam. A couple of these people were former sailing mates with whom he had not talked for decades.

And here they were - now on *his* boat!

And not just for the trip south. He would have to bring them back again that afternoon, with the kids onboard as well. At least Clara would be there. He trusted her, but as for the rest? He raised his eyebrows at the thought, continuing to stare straight ahead. It was going to be a painful day.

By 15:30 hours, the Gremlins were in a neat line on the rigging lawn at Henry's Bay, ready for the upcoming Nationals on Thursday.

It was time to head north. Back to their own Sailing Club at Banjo Point.

Crusty stood ready at the helm. He could feel himself stiffen as the noisy throng bustled along the wharf towards *Wave Leaper*. It was what it was, but having them all onboard again was stifling.

Clara jumped over the rail onto the aft deck with an enthusiastic grin, "C'mon, Crusty. Let's sail her home. This nor'easter is perfect and," she winked, "you have plenty of crew."

She looked across at Crusty. His lips were tightly pursed and then she saw his lips move, forming words with no sound.

In his mind, he was thinking, "Not sure if those kids are up to it, but if the parents stay out of the way, there's a chance."

Moving away from the wharf, with Clara at the wheel, Crusty, ignoring the dads who wanted to help, encouraged the team of young sailors to sweat the halyards, pull on the sheets and crank in on the winches.

Wave Leaper came alive. Clara could feel the power of the big ketch as she heeled over in response to the stiff breeze.

"Heave ho," commanded Crusty, as the Gremlin sailors lined up to pull on the main halyard.

The main sail was soon flapping in the wind.

Crusty shouted out, jokingly, "C'mon, my able-bodied mariners. Get that sheet under control. Yes! Billy you can do it."

Clara could not believe what she was hearing and seeing.

Crusty talking to Billy.

Billy following instructions.

Something special was happening.

The jib unfurled. *Wave Leaper* heeled over even further, water sluicing down the leeward rail as she dipped into a wave.

"Nine knots," Clara exclaimed, "and we haven't even hoisted up the mizzen sail."

Crusty punched the air. He was a real sailor and this was real sailing. The mizzen shook a few times as it was raised but as Lindy and a couple of other kids heaved in unison, the sheet tightened.

"Too much," called Crusty. "Ease a bit or she won't pull properly."

As the sheet eased, Clara felt the helm lighten beneath her grip. *Wave Leaper* was alive.

Crusty stood beside Clara, a little out of breath from the exercise.

"Well done, *yungun'*. You are steering well. I knew I could trust you with the helm while we raised the sails. It's just like a Gremlin. Feel the wind. Be the boat."

And with that, Crusty headed below, putting on the kettle for a cuppa. Clara was at the helm and he trusted her.

An hour later, with sails furled, *Wave Leaper,* neat as a pin, nudged alongside the wharf.

As the parents and grandparents disembarked, Crusty observed his *deck hands* as they scrambled over the side of the yacht and onto the wharf. He was almost smiling, having actually enjoyed the sail back to Banjo Point. The young team of sailors had come to the party, sailing *Wave Leaper* hard. Just the way he liked it!

The sailors and their families stood on the wharf, waving to Crusty, thanking him. Grunting at the parents, he had a good word for each of the sailors; something they had done, some rope they had adjusted, a knot tied. Even Billy was beaming from the compliment Crusty had given him.

When the throng had moved on, Clara helped Crusty untie and cast the lines away as he reversed *Wave Leaper* for the return to its mooring.

"Well done, Clara," he hollered, "I could not have done that without you."

Clara trundled up the hill, her heart full of smiles as she thought over the day.

The sun was shining within her even though the sun had almost set!

FOURTEEN

A coastal fog hung over the water as the young sailors, filled with pre-regatta nerves, twittered with excitement, waiting for the supposedly repaired *Pearl* to make the trip south.

Clara, bag in hand, skipped around. She was ready for today! Her preparation had been thorough under Crusty's guidance.

Wizz Kid was ready, waiting for her, glistening on the lawn at Henry's Bay Sailing Club! Crusty had promised to be there in *Wave Leaper* well before the racing started.

He would focus on Clara, analysing her movements, and, at the end of each race, share hints to enhance her performance. He promised Clara that, at the end of each race, he would have chilled water along with crunchy snack bars and fruit on hand.

The fog danced and swirled around the young sailors, leaving little droplets on the ends of their hair and eyelashes. As if from a heavy dew, the ground felt damp; footprint trails clear on the rigging lawn.

It was then that Clara noticed *Wave Leaper* was gone. The yellow mooring buoy was there, but clearly Crusty had left early. Why? She knew Crusty was different - and wise. He undoubtedly had a plan.

Clara was lost in thought. Maybe he had left early to make the best of the high tide over the shallow parts down south. But it was low tide now and any sailor would avoid the thick coastal fog, if at all possible. Adding to her worry was *The Pearl*. Her engine hatches were open and Clara could hear the engine cranking over, again and again.

A black cloud of doubt engulfed Clara. This could be a bad omen - the fog, Crusty disappearing, and now *The Pearl* unable to start again.

She squatted down on the wharf, chewing her nails, thinking.

Soon the Sailing Club's rigid inflatable rescue boats - the RIBS - were being wheeled out, fuel tanks checked and loaded, outboard engines started, smokey exhaust adding to the fog.

Three kids and an adult were a bit of a load for a rescue RIB, but there were no other options. The Banjo Point Gremlin sailors risked being late for the long-awaited National Gremlin Titles.

With noisy engines revved to full throttle and the water smooth as a mill pond, the *armada* soon disappeared into the mist. At least the water was flat. They could use their mobiles to navigate their way through the fog to Henry's Bay. Above the noise of the engine, the foghorn at Banjo Point Lighthouse could be heard moaning across the bay.

When the Henry's Bay Sailing Club finally came into view, the kids were wet and cold; their muscles stiff and sore from the uncomfortable ride. Luckily, they could see the red and white pennant - signalling postponement of the race - hanging lifelessly in the still air. They had time to warm up and to rig up.

The rigging lawn was now alive with activity. Boats were being checked and prepared. Sails raised. Rudders and centreboards polished over and over again.

At 14:00 hours, the hooter sounded. The red and white pennant slid down the pole. The young competitors had half an hour to be on the start line for the first race. By now, the fog had burned off and a steady nor'easter rippled the water.

Clara stood beside *Wizz Kid*. Looking out over the water, she was relieved to see *Wave Leaper*. And thankfully, there he was. Crusty on his deck, waiting, in anticipation of the upcoming race day.

Although Clara wished Crusty had come ashore to help her rig, she was also aware that her premonitions, thankfully, were wrong. She could feel her heart butterflying in her chest now as *Wizz Kid* floated free from the launching dolly. She jumped in, satisfied. Ready!

The start line was just north of the Henry's Bay Sailing Club. Crusty had moved *Wave Leaper* into a prime position. His goal was to clearly watch Clara, with nothing in his path.

"What happened to you this morning?" Clara queried as she passed the anchored yacht.

"Don't worry about me. I knew *The Pearl* wouldn't start and I'd turn into a water taxi again," he croaked, a voice more gravelly than usual.

In quick succession, he reminded her to "Feel the boat. Be the boat. The wind - *the wind* - is your friend. You can do this and don't forget to come back for a snack after each race."

Red curls tied in two tight pigtails against a face smeared untidily with sunscreen, Clara gave Crusty a thumbs up. Then she was gone.

By the end of the first day, Clara was ecstatic. She scored a fifth, a second and a third which probably placed her in the top four for the day. Billy, on the other hand, had a disappointing eighth, a first and then a disastrous twelfth place. Ashore, he blamed the race officer for the course, the wind for shifting and younger kids for getting in his way. He naturally was not responsible for his poor results and his single first place was proof.

Clara smiled as she listened to his crabbiness. Everybody else was at fault. He was hilarious, she thought, as he blamed his new sail for being too new!

Twilight moved toward soft grey as the summer evening gave way to night. Sleeping bags were rolled onto camping mattresses, and the kids, now in their pyjamas, teeth brushed, settled in for the night.

Clara took a last look out of the big windows of Henry's Bay Sailing Club before she settled. There, at anchor, swaying gently, was *Wave Leaper*.

She sighed. Crusty had been a great help analysing each race and giving hints and encouragement.

It just seemed *wrong* that he was totally alone out there.

FIFTEEN

Day Two of the Nationals dawned with a beautiful sunrise. Soft pink clouds covered the sky, becoming brighter as they marched towards the east. Even Henry's Bay joined in the celebration of this fine morning, reflecting the various pinkish colours shimmering off of its calm waters.

Clara was reminded of that old saying *'red sky in the morning, sailors warning'* as she soaked in the colours.

Racing was due to begin at 10:00 hours. Clara was rigged and ready, a good half an hour prior.

Just to frustrate her, the hooter sounded. The first race of the day - postponed. The red and white pennant was hoisted onto the flag pole for the second day in a row. No wind again. Luckily, though, the forecast was for a steady twelve knots by midday.

Finally, the Gremlins launched at 11:00 hours; the wind just raising a ripple on the calm sea. Starts were difficult in these conditions, but Clara had practiced.

So had Billy.

The two seemed to be able to jump out of the pack at just the right moment, leaving the other Gremlins to fight for the little wind there was. Clara could just see Lindy breaking free. Lindy had worked hard and was now in the top ten across all three races thus far.

But Billy had supposedly *forgotten* to sail the race, despite his good start. Instead, he focussed on attacking Clara's position, allowing other boats to get ahead. After the first race of the day, Clara sailed up to *Wave Leaper*.

Arms folded across her chest, she cried out in frustration, "It's so unfair. Billy is so determined to beat me that I'm losing my position in the regatta."

"That's exactly how Mark Ayers would have coached him to race. Did exactly the same thing to me in '63 and '64. I hated it, but it didn't stop me from achieving my best. Believe it or not, I actually developed clever strategies from Ayers' disruption."

"But I am with you," Crusty hollered, "I understand your frustration, *yungun'*. I feel like giving that little blighter Billy a flat nose - and one for his coach too!"

Crusty was clearly not happy, but he appeared calm, looking Clara straight in the eyes. "Now Clara, in this situation, you have to sail your own race. *Stay away from him*. Stay out of trouble. You are above petty confrontations. I have seen you sail your own race and I'm sure you can do it again. Here! At Henry's Bay!"

He smacked his hands together and then, pointing a scrawny wrinkled index finger at her, cautioned, "Now remember... the wind."

Clara grinned at Crusty, gave him a thumbs up, and was off for the next race; her cheeks full of banana and her focus renewed.

Day Two of the Nationals ended. Clara was ahead of Billy, but by the closest margin.

Billy was anything but happy. Clara, by contrast, was grinning as she settled into her sleeping bag for a second night away from home.

SIXTEEN

The forecast for Saturday was excellent. With a fifteen to eighteen knots nor'easter, this meant the racing would be fast, a bit on the edge, and for sure, capsizes would occur. Small mistakes would have major consequences.

Sailing out to the start, Clara passed *Wave Leaper's* stern.

"Perfect!" she called out, "Just what I need. This is going to be a very good day."

"A regatta is often lost on the second last day," Crusty warned, "I like that you are confident, but remain focussed. Remember all the points we've covered."

"I can't wait Crusty. This is the sort of wind I had hoped we would get."

"Still… avoid trouble, sail for the clear air and … ."

"I know," Clara butted in, "Have fun and the rest will follow."

Crusty beamed with pride in a Crusty sort of way as Clara sailed away, toes embedded securely under her straps. As the breeze freshened, she leaned out as far as she could, ably balancing *Wizz Kid*.

Clara finished the third race of the day on a high. She had achieved a third, a fourth and then a first in the last race. As she passed Crusty, she was sure he smiled.

He was certainly animated; his pigtail whipping around, his eyes bright and glistening, almost tearful. He could not stand still. His hands were flapping around as he bounced from foot to foot.

"Thanks for all your help, Crusty," Clara called out as she sailed past, "I certainly could not have done it without you."

She then doubled back, sailing past *Wave Leaper's* stern.

"Please come in for the BBQ this evening. It's open to everybody who has been involved and you Crusty - **you** - are the reason I am sailing in this regatta."

"I'll check and see if I have anything else on," smirked Crusty.

"I expect to see your dinghy coming ashore around 18:00 hours, matey!" and, with that, Clara headed for Henry's Bay Sailing Club.

Just after 18:00 hours, Crusty was preparing to tie his dinghy to the wharf. It was clear that he had taken the trouble to spruce up a bit.

Clara was watching him.

Protecting his gammy leg, he climbed onto the wharf and began fidgeting unnecessarily with his dinghy's rope.

Clara stepped toward him and gave a wolf whistle, "Pretty spiffy looking there, Crusty!"

"First BBQ I've been to in years," he said, and began fidgeting with the rope again.

"Relax, Crusty, these are good people," Clara whispered.

*

The queue at the BBQ snaked around the deck. Parents and kids lined up together, chatting enthusiastically about the successes and failures of the day. There were stories of rescues, of some of the young sailors breaking the rules and subsequent protests - who was right and who was wrong; stories of narrowly being beaten, or of managing to just stay ahead. The chatter was happy, animated, filled with laughter and cheeky comments - the fellowship evident amongst the young competitors and their families.

With Lindy next to them, Crusty and Clara chatted like old mates.

"Who would have thought it? Only a few months back you were always last," Crusty grinned at Clara.

With one arm slipped through Lindy's, Clara beamed at Crusty.

It was clear. Clara had sailed brilliantly. At the end of Day Three of the Nationals, she was the top girl and, currently, third overall.

Soon Lindy's mum and dad joined them in the queue. The Ryans, Tim and June, knew that Crusty would be feeling a bit uncomfortable. They gave him space as he awkwardly tried to join the conversation.

Crusty avoided eye contact as much as he could. Scanning the ground as if he had lost something precious, at least, so Clara thought, he was there, making an effort to socialise.

By 21:00 hours, the Club was quiet. The exhausted young sailors had settled down to sleep; many were overtired while some of them, physically drained, had become a touch emotional, tears teasing out from the corners of their eyes as they lay snuggled into sleeping bags.

SEVENTEEN

Sunday. Day Four of the Nationals. Clara woke, feeling anxious. She smacked her hands together and began to reprimand herself, "Can't believe how well this has all gone. Now don't go stuff it all up. Got that?"

During breakfast, it was announced that the first race of the last day was postponed. No wind again!

By 11:00 hours, the Gremlins had launched, but it was a confusing wind that would not settle into a consistent pattern.

Frustrated, the Race Committee had to move the course each time the wind changed direction. Gremlins were milling around the Start Boat waiting for the race course to be finalised. Rescue boats and spectator boats, loaded with parents and grandparents, hung about nearby. Waiting.

Despite the confusion, Clara was enjoying just being out on the water in *Wizz Kid.* She had sailed away from the crowd, appreciating the wind swirling round her in what looked like a stunner of a day. A cheeky gust of wind teased her, plucking her cap off her head, forcing her to sail back to pick it up.

As she scooped it up, a dark line across the water, to the west, caught her eye. She froze as fear gripped her.

Wind! but not just any wind.

A rogue westerly gale was raging across the bay towards the fleet.

Clara's heart pounded as she turned *Wizz Kid* towards Henry's Bay Sailing Club. She knew she was further out than anybody else. She could see rescue boats already plucking kids off their Gremlins, leaving their boats to capsize. There was a lot of shouting. The start horn on the Committee Boat sounded again and again. An urgent warning. The wind front had not fully arrived but you could *feel* its threat in the air.

And then the wind struck! The surface of the water upwind of *Wizz Kidd* exploded. Clara tried to maintain her boat's balance, but she was no match for the gale. *Wizz Kid* tipped over, dumping Clara into the water.

Clara quickly swum around the stern and grabbed the centreboard before *Wizz Kidd* could turn herself fully upside down. She heaved with all her might and slowly, begrudgingly, *Wizz Kidd* came upright.

Half full of water, she wallowed as Clara slipped over the side into the boat. The main sail was flapping wildly. Clara found the bailing bucket and started to furiously empty the boat.

The wind moved from a squall to a fierce gale, picking up the surface of the already breaking waves and driving a stinging spray across Clara's face. She continued to bail the water out to keep the boat upright as the sail furiously flapped in the gale. But the gale was increasing and, as fast as Clara bailed, the waves were sloshing over the side filling the boat. Despite Clara's efforts, *Wizz Kidd* slowly tipped over again. Clara was back in the water.

Once again, she swam around reaching up for the centreboard as the boat tipped further over; the mast now pointing almost straight down into the depths. Again, Clara heaved with all her might. Slowly *Wizz Kidd* came upright. The mast was now level with the water. All that remained was for one final heave. But, no luck. The wind had blown *Wizz Kid* around; her mast now pointing upwind.

As Clara pushed down on the centreboard, *Wizz Kid* slowly began to come upright. The moment the mast rose above the surface, the wind caught the sail once more, flipping the boat violently over on top of Clara. The sail landed on her head, pushing her under the water. Terrified, she swam her way up towards the surface only to see *Wizz Kidd* slowly rolling over. It was now completely upside down.

Clara tried again. Just as she was ready for the final heave, the wind slowly spun the boat around. The mast was pointing upwind once more. As Clara pushed down on the centreboard in a final effort to right the boat, the wind caught the sail and, once more, flipped the boat over onto Clara. Again, she was under the sail fighting to get free; to get air.

Each time, Clara swam clear and tried again. Each time, the boat flipped over onto her. In no time, Clara was exhausted. Eventually, the force of the gale and the weight of the boat - the fight to get it upright - took its toll. Clara could feel a cold fear rising in her.

As she bobbed around in the water, Clara tried to determine which direction Henry's Bay was, but the driving spray made it impossible to see beyond a few metres. Not even a rescue boat could be sighted; just driving spray.

"I can do this," she shouted above the wind, more to give her courage than believing that she could.

Clara tried one last time to get *Wizz Kid* to come back upright and remain upright.

As she heaved on the centreboard, a sudden creak and then CRACK! The centreboard broke off from where it entered the hull. Clara was left with the broken piece in her hand.

"Nooooo," screamed Clara, as she struggled to keep her head above the surface, "Noooo."

Without the leverage on the centreboard, *Wizz Kid* slowly turned upside down; her mast pointing towards the grey depths of Henry's Bay. And there she stayed, upside down; the crashing waves pushing her forward and back.

"Helllpp... Nooooo!" Clara was beyond calm, paddling against the pressure of the rolling waves; the driving spray biting into her cheeks.

There was so much water spraying furiously into the air that the line between under the water, in the water and above the water, blurred. Clara struggled to breathe. Her mind was spinning with possible solutions.

"I should swim. Yes. Swim to shore. That's it," her mind shouted.

But she knew the old rule: stay with the boat. She coaxed herself to stay with the boat... to stay... over and over. She knew she had to stay.

The waves were now over a metre high. As the upturned hull rocked around violently, Clara found it difficult to hang on. Gasping for air, she stayed in the water beside the hull. Then she noticed it was calm under the boat.

"That's it. Under the hull... into the air pocket," she thought.

She slipped her head under the hull, her entire jaw shivering uncontrollably. She could feel no wind now - only hear it as it howled and moaned above her, the waves crashing on the upturned hull.

Clara hung on. She was determined. She was resilient. She would shiver but she would wait. Wait for rescue or wait for the westerly to abate.

She thought half an hour passed; it seemed like more - the passage of time an unknown. Clara's hands were now white, bloodless, cold. She shivered to her very core; her old wetsuit no match for this marathon session.

Above the wind and crashing waves, she thought she heard the *duff duff duff* of a diesel engine. Soon the gratifying sound filled the upturned Gremlin. She stuck her head out to look, but driving spray beat her back under the hull.

She waited. The sound was getting closer. The fury of the waves began to abate. She popped her head out. Upwind of the upturned *Wizz Kid* was *Wave Leaper*.

"Grab this line," Crusty called as he threw her a thick rope. Hanging on to the large knotted end, Clara was dragged toward the big boat and then hauled over the gunwale and into *Wave Leaper*.

"I thought you were a goner. Now get below, *yungun'*; get dry and we'll head back to the wharf at Henry's Bay."

Shivering uncontrollably, Clara stumbled down the companionway; her legs numb with fatigue and cold. A pile of towels was waiting to warm her body. Wrapping several towels around her, she paused to hear the familiar crackle of the radio overhead.

"Henry's Bay Sailing Club. Henry's Bay Sailing Club. This is *Wave Leaper*."

"*Wave Leaper*. This is Henry's Bay Sailing Club. Receiving you. Loud and clear."

"Henry's Bay Sailing Club. I have Clara. She is onboard. Cold but warming up. Heading back now. Standing by. Channel 16."

The wind whistled through the rigging; the *chop, chop, chopping* of the waves slapping the hull. *Wave Leaper* heeled over slightly against the wind. The diesel engine thudded - a solid reassuring sound - pushing her confidently forward.

"Well, don't just stand there, *yungun'*. Pour yourself some of that warm tea from the flask," offered Crusty, as he leaned into the companionway. "We need to get back for the prize-giving and no one wants to see you up there on the podium shivering."

"Dddoes this mmmean yessssterday's ppppositions ssstand?" Clara shivered out her question.

"You bet they do. Top girl in Australia by a country mile and third overall. Fantastic result," Crusty sang out, "I knew *Wizz Kid* could do it. She just needed the right skipper to come along."

"Wwwwhat about *Wwwizz Kid*?" Clara asked, her teeth chattering relentlessly as she tried to control her breathing

"She'll be fine. Now we gotta get going... we'll collect *Wizz Kid* as soon as the wind eases, which, I reckon, will be soon."

*

It was then that Clara understood. The Gremlin National Titles was over; the stress and tension, and the long hours of preparation. The hopes and the dreams.

The results from Day 3 were standing. She *had* finished ahead of Billy - she was ranked as third place overall; Billy a bit further down the ladder. She was thrilled. Amazed. Ahead of Billy whose Pop was the Commodore. Ahead of Billy whose family had a history of sailing and a long line of successes. Ahead of Billy who was supposed to have been first. He had made that clear during practice. After all, he had a new boat - the best money could buy including new sails. And he even had a former Australian Olympic Games Coach on his side.

She looked up into the companionway to where an old leathery faced bloke with watery blue eyes and a long grey pigtail was wrestling the wheel of *Wave Leaper*. The boat crashed over a particularly strong wave and Clara was very sure she saw Crusty smile.

"How lucky I am. How good to have Crusty beside me. He is... **he is Wizz Kid**!" she thought.

Wave Leaper jarred again. The rigging whistled as the westerly blew, while a halyard clanged against the mast. Warm tea was starting to produce results. Even the mug slowed to a steady shake in her hands.

*

Mum drifted into Clara's thoughts: thoughts that she had kept at bay while she remained focussed on the National Gremlin Regatta.

She was confused and bewildered at the same time.

"Where was she? Why hadn't she come to Henry's Bay to watch the last day as she had promised?"

EIGHTEEN

After wrestling with the gate, Clara was relieved to find the front door open. Slinging her sailing bag into the hall closet, she could feel a change in her energy. Mum was *home.* She had so much to tell her.

Excitement whipping through her, Clara did not pick up in the first instance what could only be described as a disturbing quietness.

She cried out, "Mum, I won! Mum? Mum? Where are you?"

A movement on the chair by the lounge room window gave her position away.

"No need to shout, Sweetie," Mum said in a lowered, flattened voice, "I'm just here."

"Muuuummmm," Clara bounced into the living room, exhilarated. "I won. I am the top Gremlin girl sailor in the country. And I came third overall. Aaannnnnd... I *beat* Billy!"

She threw herself onto the sofa, sunk into its worn-out cushions, barely sucking in air as she continued, "*Wizz Kid* is fast - no - more. A whirlwind. Early today there was an unbelievably huge westerly.

No one could finish any race today, so yesterday's totals were used. And, Mum, I nearly died. Crusty rescued me. It was total carnage. I broke the centreboard and drifted under the boat for hours. I was literally freezing. I was blue! Blue hands... blue lips... "

Words continued to tumble out of Clara as she filled Mum in on the unbelievable events of the day; her eyes bright under her mop of red curls.

"I won! I can't believe it. I won! Mum - I got a medal. Look!" and with that she leant over Mum's shoulder and dropped the Gold Medal into Mum's hand; its green and gold ribbon streaming behind.

It seemed as though Mum had woken from a dream. She appeared dazed and confused, as if this wild red-headed child had blown in by mistake. Looking down at the medal in her right hand, she straightened the ribbon with her other hand.

"Clara, what did you win?"

"Mum... !? I sailed the National Gremlin Regatta at Henry's Bay Sailing Club. Don't you remember. I left last week... Thursday. Remember how foggy it was?"

"Oh.. Yes that! Was it fun?"

"It was fantastic. I beat Billy despite all his fancy equipment. Crusty knew I could do it. He just knew I had it in me. Crusty is a *hero* coach. And Mum... Lindy came ninth overall. She didn't even think she would make the top twenty."

"Well done, Sweetie," she murmured, motioning Clara away with the flick of her hand, adding in almost a whisper, "Please make me a cup of tea. I'm parched."

Staring at the back of her Mum's head, Clara responded, with just a hint of sarcasm, "Which type of tea?"

"Um, could you make it a Darwin Daydream, please," and then in a dull and sluggish voice, she added, "It's nice to have you back."

Clara frowned at the kettle as it began to rumble with boiling water. The unwashed pile of dishes spreading across the counter top, little pizza crusts peering out between them, told Clara everything. The place was in a mess!

"Are you going to ask me *anything* about the Nationals?" Clara shouted from the kitchen, annoyed, confused as she held back her anger.

"Oh yeh! Uh... how was it?"

Clara shook her head in disbelief. Breathing deeply, she worked to gather her self together, responding in measured terms, "Mum! I. Have. Told. You. I actually WON!"

"Did you? Well done, Sweetie. Was it fun?"

With a rising sense of desperation, Clara, clenching her fists, glared at her Mum, "Are you here? What has happened to you? You are worse than that old lady who was lost at the bus stop."

Mum slowly turned and looked at Clara.

What Clara saw shocked her.

She shrieked, "Mum! What... what happened. What happened!"

A black bruise wrapped around Mum's left eye, spreading from a purple- coloured eyelid through to a blackish hue across her cheekbone. The eye was more or less closed, although a flash of red was visible, crusty tears in the corner.

Slowly Mum's left eyelid opened, allowing Clara to see the extent of the damage done to the injured eye. Mum seemed to be *seeing* Clara for the first time; her focus steady, yet emotionless.

The kettle started to whistle and Clara, relieved to be distracted, moved out of view to make the tea.

"What happened, Mum? When did you get that shiner? How did it happen? Where were you?"

Mum didn't answer directly. Instead, she slowly turned away, mumbling, "I fell down the stairs."

"Have you been to the doctor? When did this happen?"

But there was no answer; just the reflection of Mum in the window as the setting sun made way for the darkness wrapping around the the townhouse.

Clara was afraid. Her mind whirled. She could feel her heart thumping as she worked out what she could do... should do?

Mum had not moved. She just gazed out of the lounge room window, managing just a whimper of thanks when the tea was delivered. She did not respond to any of Clara's questions.

Clara considered her options.

Seek help from Crusty or Lindy's parents or even Billy's Pop. Crusty couldn't help her - he didn't have a car. She didn't have Billy's Pop's mobile so that was out. It would have to be Lindy.

But then there would be questions - more than likely uncomfortable ones. Clara was far from ready to answer any, especially as Mum had disappeared into her own world. Clara could not make any sense of her Mum's obvious detachment. She knew with certainty that her Mum was in a mess and may have been in a mess even since Thursday, the first day of the Nationals. She needed to concentrate. Cleaning up the mayhem in the kitchen might give her the time to clear her thoughts - to think. The warm water spraying onto her hands was already calming her as she thought through the next move. A gentle conversation with her Mum was what she needed.

Her mind wandered back to a day she would never forget. She had sailed so well - and then the storm. The cold - she had never felt so cold! Ever! Bowing her head as a beautiful medal was draped over her. And then the applause.

Clara startled. Mum stood up quite suddenly.

"I'm going to bed. I have to be at work in the morning," she said slowly, softly.

Clara stepped in her way as she crossed the room.

"What happened, Mum? We need to talk. I know, and you know, that there's no way you fell down the stairs. Did someone do this? Who? Why? Mum, please... ."

Mum looked at Clara and it was again as if Clara had just arrived home. "I need a hug, Sweetie. I've got such a headache."

Clara wrapped her arms around her Mum. It was as if Mum had grown smaller. She was not the carefree and energetic Mum of even a week ago.

She could sense that Mum was tense - afraid of even being close - but Clara hung on hoping that her hug would make Mum feel better. Slowly Mum relaxed; the tension draining out of her until she was holding onto Clara in a bearlike grip as if she would never let go.

"Mum? What happened? You need help? Have you seen Dr Walker?" Clara whispered.

Mum stiffened and pushed Clara away.

"I'm not going to any doctor. And Walker will ask too many questions. Neither you nor I can afford to have anybody asking anything. Do you understand? I fell down the stairs and that's that. The past is behind now and we are going to move forward."

And with that she brushed Clara off and headed up the stairs.

Clara slumped into the nearest chair, holding her head in her hands while tears streamed down her face. She tried to make sense of the situation she was now in.

It had been a long day. A day of happiness, then fright, followed by relief as she was pulled from the surging water, and then - receiving an award. Totally unexpected. Now... this!

Clara knew that the only thing that really

mattered was to be strong for Mum. Mum needed her help.

Straightening her shoulders, Clara stood up and moved to the kitchen, resolved that she would clean up the mess of food and dirty dishes and then work on how to have a conversation - a *good* conversation - with Mum.

NINETEEN

Considering the emotional start to the week, Clara concentrated on being positive. There were no answers to her questions and Clara chose to just be sensitive to Mum's requests, eat the simple meals Mum prepared. To let things evolve.

It was Wednesday. Clara skipped down the hill to the Sailing Club.

The Banjo Point Sailing Club Twilight Race Season had begun. *Wave Leaper* was entered into the Twilight Race, the first time in many years. Crusty invited both Clara and Lindy to crew with him, but Lindy's dad Tim insisted on joining them. It didn't matter to Crusty. He had no issue with Tim Ryan. Crusty was a serious racer. He couldn't stop fiddling throughout the race. But he didn't just fiddle. He explained what each rope and adjustment did, how it would make the boat faster, or safer, or more under control.

Lindy and Clara took turns at the wheel while Crusty, like an excited kid, bobbed around from one end of the boat to another. Eyes bright, his limp was barely visible as he moved from bow to stern and back again.

Despite being older and heavier than the other boats, *Wave Leaper* had sliced through the waves and handled the currents with ease.

It was a perfect Twilight Race, filled with laughter amidst the hard work; resulting in an excellent outcome.

As they clambered off *Wave Leaper* and onto the wharf, Tim, Lindy and Clara waved a thank you to Crusty.

Crusty grinned back and, to their surprise, gave a deep bow.

*

Friday morning was the beginning of the *Learn to Sail Holiday Program.* As experienced Gremlin sailors, Clara, along with Lindy and Billy, were part of the instructional team. They gathered together in the Clubhouse and waited for Peter, who was running the program, to begin their introductory course as instructors.

He thanked the young sailors for their commitment to being a part of the *Learn to Sail* program; for being instructors for these excited *newbies.* He reminded them to stay close to the new kids, help them rig the boats, and demonstrate care when using the RIBs.

As Peter continued his introductory words, Clara's attention slipped. She found herself gazing out of the large Clubhouse window to where *Wave Leaper* was swaying gently in the morning calm. She could see Crusty, busy on board, fiddling with the mizzen sail. Up it went, some adjusting occurred, and down it came. More fiddling and up it went again.

Screeching of chairs as her fellow instructors began pushing away from the table brought Clara back to the meeting. Her sailing mates were standing, stretching, chattering. It had been a lengthy pre-orientation session and more was to come.

"Right, team, let's look at the roster and who will be in charge of what groups. Let's move on - back you get. Sit."

Peter grinned and began to discuss the rosters: who would be working with whom, emphasising that he had carefully chosen the leaders, matching their strengths, balancing their talents. A surprise for Lindy, Peter announced that she would be 2IC of the team training the youngest kids. And then a greater surprise.

"Team Two will be assisting the older students led by Billy with Clara as his 2IC!"

Peter gave Billy a thumbs up.

Billy lashed out, "No way! I want to work with Justin. And have just a boys' team."

Peter hesitated, but only briefly.

Although Billy's retort caused amusement amongst the team, Peter gave Billy a patient look, firmly declaring that, "In sailing, boys and girls are equal. As sailors, as helpers, as team mates! Work with Clara or we will find another team leader."

Billy was cross - his face creasing with angry lines, eyes squinting. He glared at Clara; frustration and resentment in his stare.

"Stupid girl!" he mouthed across the table.

Clara met his stare. A smile was her answer. She gently tapped three fingers on the table between them, and, with no words, reminded Billy that she had beaten him at the Nationals a mere week ago.

After the introductory session with Peter, Clara and Lindy wandered out of the Clubhouse, and across to the jetty. They had agreed to have some sailing time with Crusty.

In a united voice, they hollered across at Crusty, "Ahoy Skipper..." and in moments, Crusty had collected them in his dinghy.

As they rowed toward *Wave Leaper,* he gave a wrap of his morning chores, bubbling away with enthusiasm, such was his love of being back on *Wave Leaper,* preparing her to sail - to move with the wind. He was rowing with energy as he continued his soliloquy; his eyes bright and filled with a clear love for sailing.

Once onboard, he outlined carefully his attempts to ensure the mizzen mast was operating smoothy, highlighting the importance of constant maintenance. He explained to the girls how important it was to maintain the windlass, especially as it was vital for pulling the anchor chain back onboard.

The girls rolled their eyes at each other, working hard not to giggle as Crusty rambled on: how to use this, when to do that, how this system worked, what problems were most likely to occur, how to fix them!

As the shadows lengthened along the shoreline, and the lesson came to an end, Crusty rowed the girls back to the Sailing Club. They tumbled out of the dinghy and onto the jetty, their heads full of all the things Crusty said they HAD to know if they were to sail a boat across the ocean.

Waving goodbye to their mate Crusty, they were surprised to hear him say, with just a touch of sadness, "Don't forget *anything* I have taught you as you *never know* when you will need it! I may not always be here to back you up."

And with that he turned the dinghy towards *Wave Leaper*.

TWENTY

Day one of the *Learn to Sail School* had started well. A sense of fun filled the Clubhouse. One by one, mums and dads dropped off their wide-eyed children. Parents fussed around trying to make sure that their kids were in the right place. Others asked who was 'in charge as Johnny needs his puffer on hand' and 'Sally needs a second application of sunscreen in the middle of the day - she is a delicate soul'. It appeared that each child had to have special attention in some way. The now experienced Gremlin sailors watched, amusement playing across their faces, as they reflected on *their* initiation and how scary it had been for them a few years prior.

The *Learn to Sail* students were decked out in an array of wetsuits: poorly fitting new ones, old worn ones, ones that were too tight, ones too loose. Some even wore pristine white beach shoes that were just calling out for a *mudding*. Hats covered not only their heads but their eyes and faces. A motley crew for sure, but faces covered with masses of white zinc sunscreen turned the little smiles into wide grins.

Team leader Peter welcomed the *Lean to Sail* students and introduced the team members. Prior to the first lesson on how to launch a dinghy, he explained, in meticulous detail, the important safety instructions. Understanding how to keep their Gremlin safe and protected from the rocky shore was crucial.

And then it was time.

The first lesson began. How to launch a Gremlin. The *newbies* practised launching and retrieving the Gremlins until they were confident that this was one task they could do well.

The energetic young sailors were ready for the next activity: to begin the first steps in sailing. By the time the newbies were organised - two to a Gremlin - and launched on the river with their tow ropes tying them together, one behind the other, Clara, in a Sailing Club RIB, was waiting for them. As she edged away from the shore, she had the leading boat's tow rope in her hands, ready to take up the tension as she began to pull the boats along. Fussing like a mother swan, she instructed them to use the tiller to steer and follow her. They did, without incident.

Soon the centreboards were added to the task and the 'crew' now had to ensure they steered straight to avoid capsizing. The focus on following the RIB became even more imperative. Clara was sensitive toward her young learners, being careful to explain the different movements. Her 'crew' listened and responded well.

Billy, it appeared, also had a 'crew' of good potential sailors, however, Lindy's 'crew' needed far more support. The kids on her team seemed to have trouble understanding her instructions, eventually leading to two of the boats capsizing. The screeching and shrieking as the kids floundered around in the river had everyone laughing uproariously.

As the morning moved on and the sun positioned itself directly overhead, tummies were rumbling. Lunchtime! The smell of sausages cooking on the Sailing Club's BBQ drifted across the rigging lawn as the Gremlins were retrieved; each one placed neatly in a row on the lawn. The hungry younger sailors hopped along beside their team leaders, heading happily toward a well-earned lunch.

The afternoon started with rigging. First it was masts up, then sails hoisted. Despite Billy's palpable antagonism towards Clara, the pair worked well together. They were equals - this was clear - in spite of Billy's obvious arrogance. By the time the theory lesson was over, a gusty sea breeze began winding its way across the dunes: a sea breeze that would be far too strong for a new sailor to handle!

"Who's first?" Clara asked. "I will be steering and your role is to handle the main sheet."

She looked around at all the hands up. Only Sandy had hesitated, standing behind the others.

"Chicken?" Clara winked. "Come on, Sandy. *You* are first. Let's show everybody that it's nothing to be scared about."

The rest of the 'crew' sat on the rigging lawn, ready to watch Sandy and Clara. Clara repeated what Sandy needed to do, and soon they were sailing away from the shore, heading across the river.

The boat was moving quickly. Both Clara and Sandy settled onto the gunwale, balancing the boat against the wind. Clara continued giving feedback to Sandy as they tacked, heading in towards the Sailing Club. They tacked again, heading eastward.

"You're good, Sandy. Really good!" Clara chirped. Sandy turned and grinned at Clara.

"Ease!" shouted Clara, as a gust of wind whirled toward them, "Let go. Now!"

It was too late. With knuckles white from her tight grip, Sandy hung onto the mainsheet. The Gremlin slowly tipped over, tossing its sailors into the now rippling waves of Banjo River. The girls swam to the other side of the Gremlin, pulling the dinghy upright.

Clara couldn't help laughing. "Hmmmm. Sandy... uh... you needed to let go of the mainsheet. Good thing we have our wetsuits on, hey?"

Sandy, swishing her long black hair away from her face, her eyes wide, looked across at Clara. Clara laughed again as the boat came upright.

"Worst thing that could happen is a wetting. Now slip over the side into the boat and I'll hold on while you bail the water out."

Sandy began swooshing buckets of water over the boat's side. When the Gremlin was ready to sail, Clara called out, "Balance me as I climb in."

And with that, they were off sailing once more.

"Here comes a gust. Ready to ease!"

This time Sandy felt the wind, and eased the pressure. The boat responded by sailing gently along on an almost even keel.

"Excellent. You got it!"

With that, they tacked and headed back to the launching area. Clara gave Sandy a pat on the back as she stepped onto the shore. An enthused group of smiling would-be sailors held their hands up, hoping to be the next one heading out onto the river with Clara.

*

Clara could not stop grinning to herself as she finished packing away the *Learn to Sail* boats for her 'crew'. She loved the experience - helping other would-be sailors to sail. They were fun, interested, energetic and more importantly, avid learners.

The first day over, Peter gathered his team around the 'Gremlin table'. He was impressed "Well done guys. You worked with those *newbies* really well today. And well done to those that took a 'tip' in the drink for the sake of teaching our young sailors."

The team laughed. Lindy winked at Clara.

Peter continued, "Tomorrow morning, while the river is still calm, we'll actually *start* with tipping practice. As the wind picks up mid-morning, the fun will begin."

And with that the instructors pushed their chairs back and prepared to leave. Clara and Lindy laughed about some of the young sailors who had 'just got it wrong' - some worse than others - and some who had no idea at all. They chatted as they gathered their gear and reminded each other of the

Twilight Race on Wednesday. They would, of course, be racing with Crusty. They were aware that a strong southerly was predicted to come through on Wednesday evening.

Billy, standing across from them, jumped in on their conversation. An acid comment flipped from his mouth.

"Bet you two wouldn't be able to handle a southerly in that old barge. You need to be - uh - strong - and you two certainly are not! Plus old Crusty is far too old to sail that old hulk anyway. You'll probably hit those black rocks and smash the boat to bits."

"Whoa! Slow down a bit there, Billy!" warned Clara. "I recall you enjoying a sail back from Henry's Bay on *Wave Leaper*!"

"Just once - once! There wasn't another option," he retorted.

"Hey, Billy, because you're *so* strong why don't you come on Wednesday and show us how good you are. I'll ask Crusty if it's OK to bring along a potential mutineer."

"I'll check my calendar but... not sure if I can drop my standards again. However, *yunguns'*, if there is a point to prove, I'll prove it. You two are... soft... mushy. And I am happy to prove that!"

Clara smiled ruefully at Billy as he turned away from the table. That same smile that she had given him before.

The knowing smile.

The one that clearly communicated to him that she had beaten him in the Nationals and he could do nothing about it.

TWENTY ONE

Tuesday's tipping practice was filled with hilarity. This time, Clara and the team circled their RIBs around the *newbies*. They were encouraged to tip their dinghies, right them, bail the river water out, and then tip their boats over once more. Over and over and over. It was great practice and definitely confidence building.

By lunchtime, the *newbies* were considered 'experienced'. Under the gaze and assistance of their instructors, they were soon able to control the process of capsizing. The big question was 'Could they manage on their own when things went wrong?'

By mid-afternoon, the sea breeze was ripping across Banjo River. Again, like yesterday, the *Learn to Sail* kids gathered in their different groups with their delegated instructor. This time the *newbie* had to steer while their instructor controlled the main sheet.

Clara chose Sandy once more to begin this new lesson. Although Sandy was aware that she was weaving all over the place, she felt confident knowing that Clara was controlling the sail. As she steered along, she could feel herself improving. She was *feeling* the boat.

Tommy was next. He was already nervous, clambering onto the wrong side of the boat. Quickly, Clara balanced the wind's power while she instructed Tommy to change sides. He scrambled across, clumsily pulling the tiller with him. This was not good. The boat took a tight turn as the wind passed around the boat's stern.

Clara shouted "Duck!" As the boom gybed violently across the boat.

Instead of ducking, Tommy lifted his head and - whack - the boom slammed into his head. With that, the dinghy tipped.

Tommy fell apart, wailing and flapping around in the river. Clara knew his lesson was over so she righted the boat, bailed out some water and pulled the blubbering Tommy on board.

Heading back to the jetty, Tommy was pouting.

As he scrambled onto the shore, rubbing his now fast developing 'egg' on the back of his head, he shot an insolent retort back to Clara, "I'm never sailing with you again. I only want to go with Billy."

Clara ignored the comment. "OK, who's next?"

But the kids huddled together like frightened sheep. Nobody moved.

"Come on! Who can show me how it's done?" But still they huddled together.

"Samuel? Come on. You did well yesterday. Come on Sammy."

But Sammy could only look at the ground, shuffling his feet, hands limp by his side.

"Sarah, I know you can do it. Come on."

Sarah, with pleading eyes, looked at Clara, whispering, "I don't want an egg on my head."

"Just follow my instructions and we will have no problems."

Sarah edged forward.

This time Clara took more care in explaining what was going to happen, what to expect and what she wanted Sarah to do. She encouraged Sarah to give feedback. What were her concerns? Did she understand what she would need to do? Sarah nodded each time and soon they were off, skimming across the river.

Clara controlled the main sheet while Sarah steered carefully and followed Clara's instructions. Twice Clara reached back and grabbed the tiller to help Sarah regain control. The lesson was executed with precision and when it was time to return to the

Sailing Club, Sarah pleaded for one more trip across the river.

"OK," agreed Clara, "now *you* tell me what to do!"

Sarah became the skipper and beamed with delight as she gave instructions, to which Clara replied each time "Aye! Aye! Captain."

There were many trips across Banjo River that afternoon. Clara could see both Lindy and Billy focussed on their students, laughing and encouraging them. It was clear that the young students were feeling more comfortable, and indeed, confident.

And, despite Tommy's initial disaster, he volunteered for a second attempt, under Billy's command. He still struggled to handle the steering, but Billy was ready for any mishap, repeatedly grabbing the tiller and saving both Tommy and himself from yet another capsize.

The day ended happily, with exhausted but spirited *newbies* being collected by their parents; enthusiasm bubbled through the Clubhouse that afternoon.

Wednesday, despite the wind being lighter, was a forerunner to the significant southerly forecast for later in the day. Soon the Gremlins were rigged. The

Learn to Sail students launched and sailed their dinghies back and forth across the water; concerted effort from each of them written across their faces.

A much needed lunch break and soon the young sailors were back in their dinghies for to learn some more skills.

Eventually Peter signalled his team to call their students in. It was packing up time. The southerly was beginning to move toward them and would be in full swing by 15:00 hours.

And it was! By 15.20 hours, the river had turned white with foam as the fury of the wind grabbed the crests from the waves and threw them into the air; the shore surged with froth.

The young sailing students scooted down the stairs by the wharf and skipped around on the sandy beach by the mangroves. They considered themselves sailors now! Real sailors!

The wind was not just wind. It was becoming their friend. They felt its power and understood its capability.

They knew it had to be respected.

TWENTY TWO

With the *Learn to Sail* kids packed up and heading home, Clara, Lindy and Billy moved toward where Crusty, his dinghy tied tightly to the jetty, was already waiting - patiently. Despite the Twilight Race having been cancelled due to an oncoming gale, they had agreed to sail with Crusty that evening. They were now experienced sailors and they knew that the squally conditions they were encountering was not to be trifled with. They were aware that it would be dangerous, to some extent, to be on the water, but they had made a promise. A sailor's word had to be trusted.

Soon they were aboard *Wave Leaper.* They could tell that Crusty was bubbling with energy to get sailing.

"Excellent training opportunity," he beamed. "These conditions are perfect for feeling the wind and working through the twists and turns it will present. You know the old saying 'handle 30 knots and 25 is easy'. So, let's go. Let's handle 50 and 45 will feel like a magic evening on the river."

Clara caught Lindy's eye. She could see that Lindy was nervous.

Crusty continued, "I've set up three reefs in the main, two in the mizzen and we'll furl the jib down to get her in balance. Any questions?

Well, let's get to it. Your parents know you're here Lindy? Billy? Right?"

They nodded, and Crusty added, "Clara, I know your Mum said it was OK last week. Still OK?"

Clara shrugged and grinned, "Yep, and even if it wasn't, I doubt she'd notice. She's a bit lost these days."

The diesel engine chugged as they left the mooring; the rigging whistled while the waves slapped the hull.

"We'll raise the sails in the lee of the headland and then tack out onto the bay. It's going to be fun," Crusty grinned, his long grey plait whipping from side to side as he moved from the main sail to mizzen to jib.

He was fully alive - more energetic than Clara had ever seen him.

As the main sail was raised, it flapped wildly. Then, with the halyard taut and sheets pulled on, they bore away.

Wave Leaper was in her element.

"Clara, hold this course as we unfurl the jib," called Crusty. "You will feel the steering lighten as she comes into balance."

Clara held the wheel fully over to port, but *Wave Leaper* would not respond. The main sail was rounding her up. There was nothing she could do.

"Billy, ease the main sheet quickly or we are going to lose control," she cried out.

"Give the motor a burst if she won't respond," Crusty yelled from the mast, the wind blowing his words away.

Slowly *Wave Leaper* responded. The helm lightened as the jib started to draw the yacht along.

"Bit slow, Billy," Clara commented, but Billy didn't react; his fingers were white as he gripped the main sheet. He was like a *newbie* on a Gremlin.

Shaking her head, Clara shouted above the holding wind, "Relax, guys, we can control all this power."

Crusty dropped back into the cockpit, asking the crew as he went, "How's the balance? Do we need the mizzen?"

Wave Leaper was whizzing along, water gushing down the leeward deck with the rigging whistling and a halyard slapping against the mast. A corner of the jib sail vibrated in a high-pitched buzz.

The yacht was alive. It was doing what it was designed to do: being fully balanced and powering ahead.

Clara stood behind the wheel; her red curls wild in the wind. With her jaw clenched, a look of calm determination washed across her face.

They tacked. The sails thrashed wildly in the transition.

With determination and willpower, Billy worked his muscles hard as he cranked the winch. They were soon under control again.

"You're good at that Billy. To be sure, sometimes strength is needed," Crusty commented, "but what would we do if we couldn't crank it in?"

Clara looked at Lindy; Lindy glanced at Billy. Billy was focussed on his muscles!

"Ask yourself if we have too much sail up," Crusty continued. "That is always a sign. Remember the boat should never be stressed. Never! Yes, there is strain, like now, but never too much. So always reduce her sail when you are battling to control her."

A strong gust - stronger than what they had been experiencing - whistled across *Wave Leaper*. Clara responded by fighting the wheel as the wind took control of the boat.

"That's it," responded Crusty, "any more of

those and we'll need to take another reef and furl the jib up some more."

Banjo Point Lighthouse cast its first beam of light across the ocean. Crusty's crew knew that it was time to head home. Running before the wind was considerably calmer. Lindy continued to watch the wind speed meter, calling out the strength of the gusts.

"52 knots. That's the record," she chirped.

With *Wave Leaper* reefed down and now running before the wind, the gale didn't feel that strong. Nonetheless, Crusty did not want his crew to become complacent.

"Just like on a Gremlin, an uncontrolled gybe in these conditions is bad news. You could drop the mast over the side. Control! It's all about control!"

And with that, he commanded the crew to begin the gybe.

"OK, lets gybe now to make the point. Billy, you do the jib sheets. Lindy, you continue with the main. Clara, stay with steering - slowly - and make sure the others are ready when you start that turn."

Lindy put her back into the main sheet; inch by inch, step by step. She was soon panting from the exercise, but Crusty just let her carry on. It got easier as the sail lost the wind. Clara began the turn.

Billy furiously cranked in the jib and Lindy slowly eased the main out to the right position.

"Perfect," whooped Crusty, "just perfect."

By the time they had furled the sails in the lee of the headland and chugged back to the mooring, it was almost dark. Lindy's and Billy's dads stood on the end of the jetty, chatting to each other as they watched *Wave Leaper* moving towards her moorings.

Climbing into Crusty's dinghy, all three *yunguns'* looked relaxed and cheerful, enjoying the waves bouncing them up and down. As Crusty nudged the dinghy alongside the jetty, his crew clambered ashore.

Billy and Lindy wandered over to their dads.

Only Clara remained on the jetty, turning toward Crusty as she watched him row back to *Wave Leaper.*

Waving both arms vigorously over her head, she whistled to get Crusty's attention, calling out, "Thanks Crusty. A great day."

But Crusty had already melted into the oncoming shadows of the evening.

*

Clara fought the gate after being dropped off by Lindy's dad. Found the door locked. Fumbling for her key, she was aware of the darkness inside. She flicked on the kitchen light after dropping her sailing bag near the front door.

"Mum, are you there? Mum," Clara was answered by a disquieting silence.

Leaning over the kitchen bench, Clara noticed some papers clipped together bedside the sink.

On a post-it note stuck to the first page was the word *Clara*.

TWENTY THREE

Clara curled into Mum's chair, and turned towards the lounge room window. Gazing up into the evening sky, she let out a long sigh and began to read what was a lengthy letter from Mum. She sensed it was going to be bad news. Mum had been *lost* since Clara's return from the Nationals, that is, since Clara returned to find her with a black eye, and her bold-face lie!

Clara had hoped that, during those few days before the *Learn to Sail School* began, Mum would open up; tell Clara how she could help. But Mum just seemed to be lost in her own world of pain. There was nothing Clara could do to get Mum to become conscious of her surroundings; to acknowledge that her daughter was right there beside her.

And now this letter! In itself, the writing was difficult to read, but Clara persevered. She began:

"I'm sorry, Clara, I have failed you. I have not been a good Mum.

I'm sorry. I've gone to stay with your Aunt

Constance in Kernow to try and clear my head. I'm sorry to have left in a hurry. I hope to be back in a day or two... at the most a week... so please carry on like normal. Don't tell anybody - if anybody asks, just tell them I am away for a couple of days."

The branches from the shrubs scratched across the lounge room window as a strong gust of wind whirled around the garden. Clara looked up; leaves were swirling around as if caught in a mini-tornado. She pondered how Mother Nature could capture so accurately how she was feeling. She was alone - and lonely - in so many ways.

"Damn," she growled, "why couldn't I have a Mum like Lindy's, always there, always fussing, always supporting to the point of even being irritating." Even this she would have accepted without hesitation. But Mum was gone... physically, and certainly, mentally.

She read on:

"There is dinner in the fridge, but you will need to go shopping."

It was strange how Mum could be so practical, so thoughtful and yet so terribly irresponsible.

"I have left you some money on the debit card and the code is the usual one so it will work just fine. Please don't bother to ring or text me. Aunt Constance's place is out of range and I need time to sort my head out."

"That's for sure," muttered Clara as she chewed on the end of her thumb nail.

She forced herself to continue to read the note and not crumple it into a ball, despite her rising anger.

"I'm sorry to leave you like this, but, as I said, I need time away.

You are a sensible girl and with all your commitments at the Sailing Club, I am confident you will be just fine. Keeping busy is the best thing, Clara, and it's always good to read a book in the evenings."

Clara gulped. A deep sob welled up in Clara's chest. There was no one - not one soul - to share her grief. No - her anger! Another sob welled up. Clara was shaking, her fists tightly screwed into two tight balls.

"Damn! Damn! Damn you, Mum!"

By now, Clara was shaking with anger as she read what was the final part of her Mum's note.

"*I know school starts in two weeks - Year 10 - you're growing up.*
I will be home by then. **I hope.** *And of course I'll check the debit card balance if I get to town.*"

"Whhaaaatttt! This is making no sense. Home in a few days - home in a week - two weeks - and..." choked Clara, "how can *you* suggest that you would come to town and not CALL ME! NOT SEE ME! That makes no sense. No SENSE! You'll check the debit card balance. But not me. Not me - your fifteen-year-old daughter!"

By now Clara was furious. She found herself yelling at her favourite framed picture of herself with Mum, snuggled together on her tenth birthday.

"Oh Mum! You - YOU," shouted Clara, pointing angrily at the picture, "are such a... DISAPPOINTMENT! How could I be so unlucky. Pretty pathetic you are. You could have sought help - here or somewhere. Aunt Constance! She's a fruit loop. The two of you are no doubt giggling insanely.

139

Probably howling at the moon and doing hippy dances around a campfire."

Clara's rage turned to laughter as she visualised her Mum and Aunt behaving wildly as they were wont to do when together. Crazy sisters.

Smacking her hand on her forehead, she focussed on the picture again, glaring at her Mum.

"This is so disappointing. Pathetic. Now I'm the adult here. Not you. I'm the logical one. Geez, what happened to having a childhood without any cares?"

Clara stood up and headed for the fridge. Opening the door, she grabbed her so-called dinner, smirking as she read the note attached 'Dinner tonight. Love you'.

"Love," she thought, "that's a bit rich."

Grabbing a pen, Clara scratched out 'Love' and tried to write 'Abandoned'. Even the pen let her down.

Frustrated, Clara screwed the note into a tight ball and threw it into the bin.

TWENTY FOUR

Thursday dawned and as the day softly opened to a light breeze, with the sun just beginning to spread its warm colours across the sky, Clara was readying herself for the day. She couldn't wait to get out of the house; away from everything - the crappy letter, the empty rooms, pictures of her and her Mum.

She froze for only a moment; remembering there was love - once.

Banjo Point Sailing Club was her *home* now; a place where she felt safe amongst friendly people who chattered and laughed and who actually were prepared to work - together. A place where the *Learn to Sail* kids appreciated her. A place where Peter complimented her on her efforts in teaching the youngsters. She even knew what to expect from Billy and that *did* have some certainty to it.

But she knew it would be awkward to arrive *too* early. Someone would question her. She needed to follow the norm. Arrive at the same time as Lindy, act nonchalantly and pretend all is well. Maybe she should collect any remaining sausages, after the lunch BBQ, for her dinner!

Curled up onto the sofa, she gazed out of the window and watched two cockatoos dancing on the grass together. That was how she felt as an instructor. Happy.

Sadly, though, that which was bringing her comfort - her role in the *Learn to Sail* course - would end as the beginning of the school term approached.

Clara's heart swelled as she reflected on her *Learn to Sail* protégés. Their parents had thanked her at different times. Parents whose kids had mentioned Clara at home, who had said they wanted to sail like Clara, who had appreciated her care and confidence. Sandy's mum even gave her a big hug in appreciation. Clara felt a tear rise as she realised how much she missed her Mum. But she fought the tear, reminding her *self* to be strong.

Eventually, Clara wandered down to the Sailing Club. She could feel the change in her as she saw a few *newbies* clambering out of their parents' cars, Lindy waving at her, and in the distance, bobbing in the calm water, *Wave Leaper*.

*

Saturday. Her shiny Gremlin was 'waiting' for her as if to say 'let's race...I'm ready to fly'! She slowly prepared *Wizz Kid* and, as if moving in slow motion, she steered toward the start line, struggling to lift her spirit; to find the energy to race well.

She knew she had to keep up the facade of 'everything's good'; to keep any one from suspecting she was *living in crisis*.

Sunday was a long quiet day! Grocery shopping was priority. She admitted that, to some extent, she enjoyed this sense of independence. However, even though she could decide what groceries to buy, shopping for one was actually difficult. She would pick up a dozen eggs and put them back for half a dozen, constantly questioning if Mum would be home before the week was out.

Monday's *Learn to Sail* course brought a new group of kids to the Sailing Club. Clara had proven to be an excellent instructor, able to build on her mistakes and her successes of the previous week.

Filled with enthusiasm and a love for sailing, she threw herself into her role - an instructor for *Learn to Sail yunguns'*, as Crusty would say. Her zest for the role was hard to match. Her explanations of processes were clear; her demonstrations of techniques illuminated her passion for the art of sailing. On occasion, Peter would pass by, slip in comments to support Clara, knowing Clara was being precise and in the moment.

It was time to place the new students into teams. Clara became the hero for the *newbies*. Each young sailor was keen to be Clara's student, but in fairness to her teammates, the students were allocated specific groups, according to their experience with sailing dinghies.

Clara's young would-be sailors were following her every move, fully focussed and already striving to outshine each other. She was like a magnet; they loved her and felt confident with Clara. She was *their* teacher. A sense of fun was obvious but it was also clear how carefully Clara observed each of them. Importantly, the *newbies* felt inspired as they learned to sail.

By Wednesday, Clara was in her element. Lindy, along with Clara, was back on board Crusty's *Leaper*, ready for the Twilight Race. Crusty had also re-invited Billy who, surprisingly, took up the invitation. It was a good evening, with more laughter and certainly less overall tension than in the previous week. Crusty nattered about electrical systems as was his wont.

Clara was barely listening; her thoughts were on Mum. She grinned, sardonically, wondering if the two of them - Aunty and Mum - were dancing around a campfire or, indeed, howling at the moon.

*

Two weeks of living alone and the new school year about to begin, Clara faced the prospect of entering Year Ten with no support from her Mum. She missed her but she was savvy enough to know that she had to get on with life. She had to ensure that everything appeared normal. To bypass any need for anyone to ask *any* questions about her personal life.

Buying school shoes from the local Church's second-hand shop was humiliating, especially as she knew one of the women who worked there, but at least no questions were asked! She was relieved to know that the shoes she chose were in very good condition, almost new.

The debit card balance was not healthy. In another two weeks, Clara would be broke. But, instead of stressing, Clara responded to a part-time coaching position that she had heard mentioned in casual conversations at Banjo Point Sailing Club.

The Pelican Point Sailing Club needed a capable coach for their school-age Gremlin sailors. It would also mean Saturday away from Banjo Point Sailing Club, obviously conflicting with her summer sailing season. On the bright side, until the end of March - almost eight weeks away - she still had Twilight Races on Wednesday nights with Crusty. Clara knew she could do this, despite the hour on the bus each way every Saturday.

*

Pelican Point Sailing Club was a new club. An enthusiastic buzz could be felt across its Clubhouse. The building, having been designed by an architect who seemed to have a feel for sailing and all it involved, had been recently completed. The boat shed was under the Clubhouse, a huge, cavernous space that still smelled of fresh concrete. It was bright, breezy, with well-designed racks for storing the dinghies.

The Gremlins were new. The coaching boat a dream. This was perfect for Clara. She threw all her energy into sharing the skills she had developed - to feel the wind and be the boat. The kids warmed to her quickly and in no time she felt appreciated - an important and sustaining factor that kept her buoyant, positive and focussed. Within a week of coaching at Pelican Point Sailing Club, and despite the excellent part-time wage she was already receiving, the Club offered her a raise if she promised to finish the season with them. How could she refuse?

*

The long bus ride home after each coaching session became depressing - far too much time to reflect on her situation and Mum. She tried reading to pass the time, to keep her mind focussed on something else, but reading and motion made her dizzy. She would try closing her eyes but the memory would always return - Mum, slunk into the armchair, not knowing what she was doing, confused, mentally unstuck, and barely registering that Clara was with her.

Questions about Aunt Constance would stir around in Clara's mind - was she good for Mum? The most worrying image for Clara was the unanswered question of how did Mum get that shiner, and more importantly, who did it? Clara was determined that Mum had suffered physical abuse. Was it her dad?

Mum would never talk about Clara's dad. She would mumble that he was a dead loss; that it was better not to even think that he *ever* existed. Conversation never extended beyond those comments.

Clara had her own questions. Was her dad paying maintenance? And if so, how? Certainly not into the debit account Mum had given her. Did he even know where Clara was? Did he know that Mum had abandoned Clara? Did *he* give Mum the shiner? Was he the reason for this shift in her life?

Clara wondered how she could contact her dad. If she could! There was her potty Uncle, her Mum's brother, who lived further up the coast. Story had it that he and her dad had been mates and that's how he had met Mum. Her Uncle had been to jail for managing to steal a pension from the government for five years before they caught up with him. He was living on a small holding; a few pigs and a chicken that, so the story goes, could talk to him.

Clara could only shake her head, "Why were there so many crazies in her family?"

After each fulfilling coaching session, slinking back into the shadowy, almost murky, home was uncomfortable, but Clara knew it was inevitable. At least for the moment. She would scratch together some food and spend the rest of the evening collapsed in front of the television. Although homework and diving into a good read kept her focussed after a coaching session, slumping in front of the TV was a better option. Often, on these occasions, she would fall into a deep sleep, only to wake in fright, finding herself chilly and achy... the television blaring. She would drag herself up to bed; the darkness surrounding her like a dense fog.

On Sundays her attention was directed on those things that needed to be done each week. She would rise early to do her grocery shopping in order to avoid meeting anyone she or her Mum knew. It was salient that she needed to circumvent any uncomfortable questions. Clara would quickly bundle the food and other necessities into Mum's shopping trolly and trudge home. This was also the day for washing clothes and bedding and towels, cleaning the kitchen and bathroom, sweeping the floors, ironing her school uniform... and then homework and Sunday was over!

"School...," Clara reflected, "miss being back in Year 9. Miss Lindy."

Lindy and Clara shared most of their classes in Year 9, often sitting next to each other, feeding off each other's energy. Now in Year 10, they only shared a few classes but they would catch up every lunchtime. Lindy seemed to always have more than she could eat. It became normal to share with Clara, who was vigilant about not raising any suspicions about her *new lifestyle*.

Lindy never asked about Clara's Mum, never queried anything as far as Clara was concerned.

Clara had perfected signing her Mum's signature to the notices the school continuously handed out: excursions mainly. Thus far, she was never questioned and she felt, to some extent, safe; the knowledge of her being alone tucked safely away within herself.

There was however one obstacle on the horizon. As it was the beginning of Year 10, the fourth Friday of the school year was the official Parent-Teacher Night. Parents or guardians had to be there. Clara knew she was heading for trouble. Each plan she concocted had a flaw. She would be found to be living alone. The final option was just to claim that Mum was sick on the night; to write a carefully scripted note to give to her pastoral care teacher.

It didn't work! The following Monday, Clara was called out of her Geography class and requested to report to Mrs Godfrey, the Deputy Principal. The

Deputy had phoned Mum's mobile to receive only voicemail responses. Contacting her workplace, the manager merely noted that Ms Tage was away on sick leave and not expected to return in the near future. A subtle comment was made that she indeed may have headed off into the hinterland and was not expected back at all. Clara knew nothing of this as she entered the office.

Mrs Godfrey was an imposing woman; tall, with grey hair tied tightly in a bun. Many of the students referred to her as 'the dragon'. Without even a greeting upon Clara's arrival at her door, or an offer for Clara to sit, Godfrey stood, hands splayed on her shiny desk, staring straight at Clara. No smile. No warmth.

"I expect you to tell me the truth, however difficult it may be for you, Clara. Honesty is one of our school's virtues. A caring school environment - one of our mandates. Now, we can NOT care for you if we don't know what's happening in your home life. And lying will make it very *very* difficult for you."

Clara didn't know if Mrs Godfrey was a person to be trusted. It was well known she ran on the principle of 'guilty until proven innocent' and the evidence had to be watertight.

"Well out with it, girl. Where is your mother? I gather your father is not - has not - been around."

Clara wiggled her toes in her second-hand school shoes. If only she could tap her heels and *poof* - she would be gone.

Lifting her gaze from her shoes to Mrs Godfrey's stare, she calmly and matter-of-factly noted, "I'm not exactly sure."

"Well! Really! When did you see her last? This is a question that requires an HONEST answer, Clara."

Clara could feel her freckles beginning to redden. She knew she had to control her anger. She knew, no matter what she said, it was unlikely to go well.

"I last saw her this morning," Clara lied, "I presume she is at work."

"Ah hah!" exclaimed Mrs Godfrey, fingers still splayed like talons, as if ready to pounce. "Your Mum's workplace, the Post Office, notes that she has been away for weeks. Now start again and this time tell me the truth, young lady! Where is your mother?"

"I don't know," Clara gulped, looking down at the carpet and wondering why the pattern was so ugly.

"Right! If you don't know where she is, then who is looking after you?"

There was a long pause.

"Well, speak up girl! No need to get tongue-tied now," Mrs Godfrey demanded.

Clara steadied her gaze and in an even tone, stated, "I'm looking after myself!"

"Disgraceful!" shouted Mrs Godfrey. "Fifteen-year-old girls living alone! Are you aware that it is against the law? And totally outside the mandate of the Child Protection Act. Are your parents that irresponsible? And you, Clara Tage, are implicated because *you* have not been honest. Go straight back to class... immediately. I will check that you are there. Now move it."

"But Mrs Godfrey, I am doing fine. I don't need any help. I don't *need* anybody hanging around. I am safe. Managing quite well. My school work is not suffering and I am on time and look at me... clean, healthy and besides... Mum said she'd be back any day now."

"You might say this but the fact remains - this action is against our statutory family welfare laws. We, as *your* school, are a Child Protection Agency and you *need* protection."

With that, Mrs Godfrey reached toward the phone on her desk, and requested that her assistant accompany Clara back to her Geography class.

Clara slipped into class, thankful that Lindy was there. Lindy whispered, "What happened?"

"Nothing, really," Clara whispered back, and opened her laptop.

"But you look like you were attacked. Your freckles are really bright - and I know you, Clara. I know something's up."

"Hey girls, settle down," Mr Newbury demanded and then stopped, stared and asked, "Are you Ok, Clara? You just look like... there's trouble... are you unwell?"

Clara hung her head, letting her curls bounce around her face, her freckles warming up again, mumbling, "I'll be fine."

She knew the situation she was in was pretty close to disastrous. There was nothing she could do to prevent it.

The last lesson for the day was close to being over. Clara could feel herself holding her breath. Had she escaped further interrogation? Convinced Godfrey that she was quite capable of looking after herself?

At that moment, Clara looked toward the door and gulped. A tall shadow, reflecting off the classroom door's window. Mrs Godfrey entered.

"Excuse me, Ms Whitby. Clara please!" And with that she waved her hand in the direction of Clara; a wave that told Clara to move it - now!

Clara rose, giving Lindy a quick glance, trying hard to look relaxed. She grabbed her backpack, shoved her book and laptop into it, and left the classroom.

The passage to the Deputy's office seemed longer than usual. Mrs Godfrey's shoes gave that particular brisk clickety-clack that comes with importance.

Clara felt afraid. Really afraid. More afraid than she had been when *Wizz Kidd*'s centreboard had broken in that storm. More afraid than ever, and she thought she knew why.

TWENTY FIVE

The Deputy Principal's office seemed darker to Clara than a few hours ago. Clara could barely make out the features of a woman seated near Mrs Godfrey's desk. As Mrs Godfrey took up her position of power behind the desk, she motioned Clara to enter.

Leaning forward she announced, "Clara, this is Mrs Small from the Department of Community Services. She deals with your sort of situation and so I need you to speak with her. A private conversation outside of the school!"

Clara's eyes adjusted to the light and indeed Mrs Small lived up to her name. Not only 'small' but short as well.

She smiled, "Hello Clara. I'm here to help. My role will be to ensure you are properly cared for until such time as we can sort out a few of the issues you are facing."

And with that she stood up, thanked Mrs Godfrey and beckoned Clara to follow her out of the office, out of the school gate, toward her car.

Once out of the school and away from Mrs Godfrey, Mrs Small relaxed. "Call me Sam. I'm a social worker. That was a tough gig in there. The Deputy is hard - a bit of a 'battle axe'."

Clara smirked.

"Jump in, Clara. Let's go find a place to have a chat. How about a milkshake near Banjo Point Lighthouse? There's a great café in the old keepers cottage with a good view of Henry's Bay and the ocean. Yeh? Good. Let's go."

Clara could feel herself dropping her guard, accepting Sam's hospitality. She knew the place well and loved the fantastic views over the ocean, across the dunes, and all along the coastline toward Henry's Bay.

Sam proved to be a person with whom Clara felt she could relax. A warm and caring smile, she was a chatterbox. Sam asked scores of questions in such a way that Clara felt no fear, yet there was still a lingering sense of nervousness. She knew she had to trust Sam, yet she felt she needed to be wary.

As she slurped down her creamy vanilla milkshake, Clara began opening up despite, at times, being hesitant. The stories Clara was sharing could possibly stack against her. Possibly against her freedom.

Sam was taking notes while asking leading questions. She would even laugh at some of her questions, admitting that she didn't like to ask so many questions, but she did have an obligation in terms of working through solutions for Clara.

"An ice cream, Clara? Choose what you want. It's on the DOCS account so go wild."

"Can I hold you to that later?" grinned Clara, patting her tummy.

"Yep, sure," nodded Sam, giving Clara a thumbs up.

As they walked back toward's Sam's car, Clara asked, "But what does all this mean? What is likely to happen to me?"

"In cases of abandonment - that is how we are viewing your situation - it will *probably* be recommended that you be placed in a foster home until you are eighteen years of age. But it's a lengthy process."

Sam paused, looked out over the ocean, seeming to see more than just the puffy pink clouds near the horizon. Finally, she returned her gaze to Clara.

Reaching towards Clara, she stroked her arm, saying, "If we can find your Mum... convince her to come back... the whole case *could* be dismissed. This does take awhile. In the meantime, until everything is sorted, is there someone you would prefer to stay with or are you ok for a social worker to be with you during the evenings and weekends. I will do my best to look after you, but it's not all up to me."

"Oh, and an important thing," she paused, unlocking the car doors, "a very important thing, is to not tell anyone anything. You have to carry on. Nothing is to change. This is now a legal case and there will be an official investigation. Your Mum could be charged. It's complicated, so it is better to keep quiet while we work things out."

Clara struggled to absorb what she was hearing. Within a short while, her life was changing again. She pulled out her phone and called Lindy. She would tell her that her Mum was away and could she stay for awhile. Her 'Mum's friend', Sam, would drive her over. A white lie but she had no options.

*

As they pulled up in front of Lindy's home, Sam helped Clara transfer her backpack and small suitcase to the footpath.

Grinning, she advised, "Now stay out of that dragon's office and I'll text you tomorrow at lunch.

Maybe we can catch up on that ice cream you missed today."

"Thanks, Sam," Clara smiled, and headed toward her *new* abode, as Lindy's mum, June, waved to her at the front door.

Once inside, Lindy's mum had a sense that something not quite right had happened. She tried to probe without being too nosey.

Clara could only shrug her shoulders and smile. She did not want to engage in another lie and could only reiterate that her Mum had to visit her sister in the country for a few days.

"Clara, it's alright. As Lindy let you know, we are very happy to have you stay with us," Lindy's mum reassured, "Lindy will be home within the hour, so why not just sort your gear out, set up your room... and then, when both Tim and Lindy are home, we will enjoy some roast chicken and chips for dinner. OK?"

"Thanks, sorry. Thanks again, Ms Ryan - er - June."

Rolling her small suitcase across the wooden floor, Clara moved toward the room that June had indicated. Things were changing - quickly.

Just when she felt she was making headway another obstacle was placed in her way.

TWENTY SIX

At the start of the school day, Clara wandered into her home room. Mr Luigi, her home room and Legal Studies teacher, was engaged in what seemed to be an amusing story with two of her classmates.

An energetic Italian who spoke with a slight accent, he had a good knowledge of his subject. Some of her classmates were convinced that he had acquired such knowledge from being on the wrong side of of the law. As the students greeted each other, Mr Luigi took their attendance, and then asked them to pay attention. He had an idea.

As it was early in the year, he wanted the group to begin thinking about the charity they would focus on. He strongly urged them to consider homeless children, and wrote onto the whiteboard a few charities that they might consider.

In his typical Luigi way, arms spread as if he was a showman, he said, "OK, here is the short list for charities that work with homeless kids."

Looking straight at Clara, he asked "Hey Clara, which one sounds good to you?"

Clara stiffened. She stared in defiant silence. Sam had said no one was to know, so why was Luigi expecting her to answer. She could only assume that Mrs Godfrey had announced to all the staff that Clara was under investigation.

From then on, Clara felt as though she was being perceived as a delinquent. She felt that her teachers knew about her situation - her homelessness! She became sensitive to how different teachers were treating her; some were gentle and caring towards her, some were uncomfortable - treading carefully as they asked her opinion or response to questions and ideas.

Or so she thought!

She really did not care. She even felt that Ms Sweatman (usually called Sweaty) was fixedly staring at her as the class, in unison, was reading a section of text together.

What Clara did not know was that no one knew. No one!

During recess, Lindy asked again, "Everything OK? You look tense, buddy."

Clara answered with a 'can't tell - won't tell' shrug and Lindy knew that she had to step back. Soon they were chatting about Wednesday evening

162

and wondering what Crusty would be wound up about this time.

At lunchtime, Clara's mobile pinged. Pushing her bag into her locker, she grabbed her mobile from her back pocket.

A message from Sam greeted her, "Pick you up after school. Same spot."

"OK!" Clara immediately messaged back, restraining herself from texting anything more.

*

Banjo Point Lighthouse Café was on the headland behind the towering red and white beacon. Clara and Sam settled themselves at an outside table beneath a beach umbrella.

Sam talked.

The sea was oily as Clara gazed towards it. Listening.

She broke the chocolate outer layer of the double chocolate ice cream into her mouth. A sense of foreboding was building in Clara. Something in Sam's composure didn't seem quite right.

"Now down to business," Sam announced, as Clara licked the wooden ice cream stick.

"The Department is aware of your Mum being in Kernow. She is claiming unemployment support so she visits the office in that district every two weeks. Your dad is paying maintenance into a bank account each fortnight. But Clara - *y*ou should not... *should not* ... make any effort to contact him. Understood?"

"Sort of," Clara whispered, "but why hasn't Mum contacted me?"

Clara took a deep breath and continued, "She's been gone for over six weeks now. My mum is such a failure. Such a total disappointment."

Sam looked up from her notes, giving Clara a stern look.

"Don't *ever* feel or say that Clara! Two reasons. One - your Mum has her own issues and is doing the best she can. It may not be easy on you but you have to let her be for the moment. The second is between you and me. If you show any cracks of frustration, any anger towards your Mum, I have to note it down and it becomes part of the case *against* you should your mum return. I never heard what you just said. Think about this. You are, in so many ways, a strong and independent person - sensible - and I'm sure you know what I mean."

Clara turned and looked south toward Henry's Bay Sailing Club. The cumulous clouds were billowing up slowly into a thunderhead; the evening sun colouring them a soft pink across their cotton candy plumes while its black base grew deeper and heavier as if straining to touch the ground. She could see the rain; its slanting lines telling her that the storm was approaching.

"So Sam, you mean that I can't tell you what I really think. What. I. *Really.* Think! At the risk that it will be used as *evidence.* Really? That may go against my receiving the best outcome? I **don't** believe this," Clara hissed.

"Clara, please understand. For your sake - to ensure we get the very best outcome for you - and your Mum - I have to assess your situation and make a recommendation to the magistrate."

Clara persisted, her anger beginning to rise, "So, Sam," Clara paused, I can't really talk to you - really. Honestly?"

"This is hard, Clara. In my experience as a social worker, it is my role to protect you as a young person in the best way we, as a society, know how. I have to analyse all the evidence presented as part of your case and suggest the best way forward."

*

Suddenly the wind over the bay changed direction, pushing the rain toward Banjo Point. The storm moved rapidly toward the Lighthouse. The grumble of thunder could be heard above the warm wind that smelt of rain. Within seconds, a ferocious gust whipped across the Banjo Point Lighthouse Café. The girl who had served Clara and Sam was struggling to fold the umbrellas away.

"Lets go in before we get blown away," Sam said, hurriedly gathering her notes and laptop and grabbing her handbag.

Clara followed, backpack slung over her hunched shoulders, dragging her feet. She was agonising over her ability to trust Sam and what she could really share with her now. What about her coaching at Pelican Point? Should she tell Sam about Crusty or would she consider him to be a danger? What about the Sailing Club and her friends there? How much did Sam know already about Clara and her activities?

"How about a hot chocolate, Clara?" Sam offered brightly, seemingly unaware of the tension in the air as they settled into a corner window of the café, watching the storm gathering momentum as it hustled across the bay. The far shore had long since disappeared into the driving rain.

Clara, ignoring the hot chocolate offer, shrugged her backpack off and cast it onto a spare chair before responding, "What is the best outcome for me, Sam? What is likely to happen to me. You are offering me hot chocolate and ice creams; getting me to talk. Yet I need to know what I can actually share.

She paused, trying to control her emotions, and continued, "I don't know what is going to happen - what *can* happen. Can't you just *leave me alone?* Just let me stay at Lindy's. Forget you ever heard about me."

As tears welled up, Clara wiped her arm across her face and looked away.

Sam reached across the table toward Clara who quickly shoved her chair back.

"Sorry, Clara, but please understand that I'm a social worker - you are *my* case. I have to look after *your* interests in the best way possible and," she sighed, "I have no alternatives. I have to present, to the powers that be, a recommendation."

"OK! What do YOU recommend?" Clara demanded, as her anger flared.

A sheet of rain hit the window. Clara waited. Sam cleared her throat.

In the quiet that followed, Sam calmly noted, "I'm going to strongly recommend, for your safety and for your health and well-being, that you are placed with a foster family until you are eighteen."

Clara's jaw dropped. She could feel her freckles reddening; the tears now uncontrollably streaming down her face.

Clara dropped her head onto her arms, "And I thought I could trust you!"

Sam's eyes showed no emotion. Her warmth and friendliness gone, she had collected the information she needed. There was no longer any need to pretend. Clara would become a ward of the state and be placed in a foster home: the only option unless issues with Clara's mother could be resolved.

Clara stood suddenly, defiance written across her face, yelling, "Thanks for nothing. Go to hell. I trusted you."

Grabbing her phone, she ran toward the door, flinging it open, letting the wind push its way into the cosy café. Without looking back, she raced out into the driving rain.

Clara ran. She ran from that 'smiling' case worker who was trying to lock her up. She ran past the base of the lighthouse that was now flashing in the darkness of the storm. She stumbled down the steep path, jumping steps, as she headed towards the black rocks where, so many months ago, Crusty's boat had almost been wrecked.

She ran. The rain pelted down, blurring her vision. A cobweb wrapped over her face. She stopped only for a moment to wipe it from her face. And she was running - hard - again. She tripped over a tree root in her path, landing face down in the soft wet sand. For a moment she lay there, sobbing, before she heaved herself up and continued to run. She could feel the wind through her now soaked clothes but still she ran. Her chest ached. A stitch in her side made breathing difficult. But she ran through the pain, along the coastal path that skirted the mangroves, towards the Banjo River Sailing Club.

Lightning flashed as she passed the parking area; the thunder roared seconds later. Clara didn't hesitate, she ran on.

She ran past the front of the Sailing Club, and gasping for breath, she slowed down as she crossed the rigging lawn. Nearing the jetty, Clara could see a light onboard *Wave Leaper.* Crusty was home.

At the end of the jetty, she took a deep breath and yelled for Crusty with all her might. He was the only person she trusted. She had to ask him what to do. He would know.

Like a hunted deer, eyes wide with fear, panting, she screamed again, "Crusteee…. Cruuuussstteeee. Heeeeeelp!"

She continued yelling, her voice lifting an octave as she fought the wind.

"Cruuuustyyyy!" she screamed again. No answer come from *Wave Leaper.* The driving rain and blustery wind swallowed up her cries.

Headlights flashed across the treetops as a car turned into the road down toward the Clubhouse. Without a moment's hesitation, Clara jumped into the dark waters of Banjo River. Her school pants washed against her legs as she swam; her second-hand shoes sloshing uselessly around her feet. Fighting against her clothing, she swam as fast as she could, determined to make it to where Crusty was moored.

Lights flashed across the water as she reached the stern of *Wave Leaper.* Slipping around to the other side to avoid being seen, she waited in the stormy darkness, bobbing up and down with the waves, in time with *Wave Leaper.*

She could still see car lights beaming in the parking lot of the Clubhouse. She knew it was Sam.

She knew Sam was searching for her. And then a thought flashed across Clara's already panic-filled mind. How did Sam know to come to the Sailing Club?

"Sam was shrewd alright," Clara thought. "She knows a lot more about me than she's let on."

Clara could just hear a car door slam above the wind and then she saw a blur of red tail lights through the trees. Sam was driving away.

Clara banged on the hull of *Wave Leaper* with her fist. She tried to yell for Crusty but knew she was struggling against the howling wind and the lashing rain.

And then, a soft light flooded the area as the hatch opened.

"Crusty," she called again, "here... here... I need a hand."

"What the dickens!!! Clara...", he yelled, as he reached over the side and helped Clara scramble over the rail, "what are you doing swimming out here in a storm? Ridiculous. Never have I ever seen anything so stupid in my life. What are you doing, *yungun*? Get down below. Talk to me... let's get some sense out of you."

The cabin was warm and dry except for the puddle Clara was making. The air was filled with the warmth of a stew that bubbled on the stove.

Safe inside, Clara shivered as the rain beat heavily against the hatches and the familiar moan of the wind in the rigging sang out.

Crusty's watery eyes were wide, "What the dickens are you up to?" he demanded as he passed Clara a pile of towels.

"This had better be a good story. Something serious must have happened to get you out here. Look at you. Wide-eyed and shivering. Swimming in the river in a thunderstorm in the dark? C'mon *yungun'*... what the hell is going on!"

But Clara could only choke back her words; tears flowed in rivulets down her face. Emotions, that she had worked hard to control, unleashed. She could not respond to Crusty.

"Settle down, *yungun'*," Crusty gently uttered as his gaze softened, "I'm not cross with you. Just... it's not... well people don't go swimming in a thunderstorm for the fun of it; less so in the dark. Now how about some tea and then we can get to the bottom of this story."

Tea was Crusty's solution to almost everything.

"Cuppa tea?" he said, "Then we'll know what to think."

And this time, more than ever before, it was probably true.

TWENTY SEVEN

Crusty listened. Clara needed to tell her story - HER STORY!

She began by relating how Mum had been a little 'off the planet' for a few years... life with Mum had begun to change.

She confided in Crusty about the past few weeks telling him about Mum's bruising, her lying and then her leaving. As she told her story, Crusty remained passive, showing no emotion. Just listening.

She told Crusty, in detail, about the manner in which Mum ignored any help from Clara and how she was dismissive of having any conversation about anything. Even hugging her brought out limited response.

She shared the situation she faced coming home after the Twilight Race six weeks ago. Mum gone. The letter. The instructions to not contact her. Leaving a debit card. Mum had all but closed the door on Clara! Then there was Sam, the social worker!

Looking at Crusty, Clara shook her head and shrugged her shoulders. She had no idea what to do next. Crusty looked deeply into her wide open eyes. He praised her for her courage in throwing herself off the jetty and swimming valiantly toward *Wave Leaper*.

"And then you looked at me like I had jumped out of .. out of ... cheese," she exploded in laughter, remembering his astonishment. "When you saw me in the water, you really thought I was some water troll. You should have seen your expression."

And then she stamped. Stood up.

"Damn! My mobile. It will be wrecked by now. It's been in my pocket." Clara wrestled it out of her back pocket and groaned.

"Quick - give it to me. We'll rinse it. Dry it. There's a chance."

After a fresh water rinse, Crusty put the phone in a bag of dry rice to absorb the water, shook it around and announced, "Good as new tomorrow, I reckon. But no guarantees," and with that he laughed as he carefully placed it on the shelf above the chart table.

"Now, let's be rational for a moment. There are problems. Some short term. Others... well they are bigger. So, in the short term, you need some stew. If you want to change into at least one of my woolly jumpers, feel free. Doubt any of my pants will help but we can tie them up with some rope."

The early evening storm had passed and, with open hatches, a warm fresh breeze filled the yacht. The sky was now a glowing sunset; the stormy darkness disappearing across the Banjo River.

*

Clara took a quick shower, knowing it would be cold as the yacht's motor was not running.

Crusty rinsed her clothes and wrung out the water as best he could, pegging them to the rail to dry.

Clara, dressed in a pair of Crusty's wet weather dungarees, pulled an old jumper of his over her head. She looked almost normal for a sailor as she sat at the saloon table tucking into Crusty's potato, beef and vegetable stew. If there was one thing Crusty was really good at cooking, it was stew.

Wiping his mouth with the back of his hand, he watched as Clara literally wolfed down not one, but two, servings of stew.

He grinned at her, as he congratulated himself, "That was good even if I must say so myself."

"Now, the second problem is," Crusty announced, "I don't think you can keep running. I can't hide you here for long - in fact, at all - and the police take *missing children* cases very seriously. In no time, they will be crawling all over the place."

"The situation," Crusty continued, "is difficult. The best option is that we let Lindy and her parents know you are here and safe. You will stay the night... we can ask them to pick you up early tomorrow morning. You can change and head to school with Lindy. Keep things ... uh ... normal. The Ryans and I can approach the authorities and see what happens next. At the moment, you are still being cared for by Tim and June until the next step is finalised. It will give all of us time to think."

"But what if DOCS insist that I am to move immediately to a foster family? What if the foster parents live far away from the Sailing Club? From my school? Far from my coaching at Pelican Point? I PROMISED to finish the season there and a sailor's word needs to stand, Crusty."

"Slow down, *yungun'*. We can't solve problems that we don't know we've got and we don't want to waste energy on problems we may never have."

"Now, it's getting late. Take yourself into the cabin up front. There's a duvet. Snuggle up and get some sleep if you can. Don't worry about tomorrow. We'll worry about that later."

With that, Crusty shut down the conversation, and started turning off cabin lights. He had a few quiet calls to make before retiring himself, one to let Lindy and her parents know that Clara was safe and would stay the night and another to the Water Police to give them a heads up.

Clara felt safe. She was beginning to see reason and to believe that the best option for a difficult situation would be found.

*

Clara woke to the sound of an inboard diesel engine alongside *Wave Leaper.* The yacht rocked slightly as the wash from the approaching vessel hit the hull. As she rose and stretched, she could hear the morning chirping of the water birds and then a somewhat stern, crisp voice stating, "John Brenton, we believe you maybe hiding a... uh... fugitive."

These were not the words Clara wanted to wake up to but she thought she recognised the voice. Could it be Sandy's dad who had been at *Learn to Sail,* watching his daughter over that January week. Or was she wrong?

Crusty winked at the Water Police Officer, "No fugitives here, mate. Just a young lady in a difficult situation. Good to see you, Joe."

Clara listened to the conversation above her while she gathered up her almost dry uniform and mobile. No matter what, she knew that Crusty would protect her. He was wise - something so many members at the Club had failed to accept. His logic would calm any situation.

"I have Clara here. Have you come to give her a lift on the School Water Bus?" grinned Crusty.

"Exactly what we were planning," the Water Police Officer, Crusty's mate, Joe Peters, quipped. "Sounds like the situation got out of hand yesterday with DOCS and the best thing to do right now is to get Clara's world back on track."

As Clara clambered up the companionway, Joe looked gently towards Clara, and said in a fatherly tone, "Come on, Clara, we will swing past Lindy's place - they know you are safe. You can change, grab your school gear, and get there before the bell. But we gotta be quick. Lindy says to tell you she has your backpack."

Joe was indeed Sandy's dad. He thanked Clara again for looking after his daughter at *Learn to Sail* and how Sandy just couldn't wait for her birthday as she was hoping to get a Gremlin to race. He then explained what would happen next.

"Over on the jetty is Officer Stannard - Maryia. She will drive you to Lindy's so you can get dressed for school, as planned, and then discreetly drop you off. As a plain clothes officer, no one will be the wiser. Until such time as DOCs has established where and who will be your foster parents, you are able to remain with the Ryans. We are just awaiting official confirmation. C'mon, climb on board, mate."

Clara heaved herself onto the Water Police Boat, mobile and crumpled uniform in one hand; a touch bewildered, a touch nervous, but in control, emotionally.

As they came alongside the jetty, Maryia, dressed in jeans and a colourful t-shirt, held out a hand to steady Clara while she stepped ashore.

Things were looking up, Clara thought as they drove to Lindy's place. Passing her home along the way, Clara gazed out of the car window and wondered if it could be called home anymore?

Maybe now she was *officially* homeless.

TWENTY EIGHT

After school that day, Officer Stannard drove Clara to her home so that she could gather up what she felt she needed in order to move forward over the next few weeks. Shoving clothes, toiletries, a few books, her wallet with that debit card, and the framed picture of Mum and Clara on her 10th birthday into a large duffel bag, Clara was ready to move in with the Ryans. She began to feel a heavy weight lift from her shoulders; indeed, from her heart.

Lindy's mum welcomed Clara with a big warm hug. With her arm around Clara, she walked her to her room. Dragging her duffel bag across the floor, Clara could feel her emotions rising, remembering that last hug with Mum.

"Will give you some space to get yourself together, Clara. Lindy and Tim will be back from the shops," she winked, "and it will be time for dinner!"

Clara moved across the room and dropped her bag, thinking how lucky Lindy was to have a family who cared about her. She wondered if Lindy considered herself fortunate indeed to be provided for so utterly well. After unpacking her *life,* Clara was called to dinner.

The dinner was a warm and comforting, the conversation encouraging as Tim reiterated that he and June were happy to have Clara stay as long as she needed to. It was wonderful to be there and Clara felt very fortunate.

*

A week went by. Clara and Lindy walked to school and returned each day, arm in arm, chattering and laughing. They worked together on homework. Sailed with Crusty on Wednesday. Saturday saw Clara heading off to Pelican Point Sailing Club to train her young sailors, while Lindy headed to Banjo Point Sailing Club. Life, for Clara, was becoming better than normal.

Another week slipped by. There was something magical about their relationship. The girls seemed to draw energy from each other in so many ways - cracking the Maths exam that they had studied for together and, unbelievably, Lindy beating Billy at a Saturday race for the first time. By the end of the third week with the Ryans, Clara could feel that dark cloud of despair lifting and, quite possibly, disappearing from her life. She understood what 'lightness of being' meant and proceeded to adapt the idea into one of her creative pieces required by her English teacher.

On Thursday of their fourth week together, the girls opened the mailbox as usual before entering the house. There it was! A letter in a DOCS envelope. Approaching Lindy's mum, who was preparing the evening meal, Clara handed the letter to her.

Wiping her hands on a towel, June tore it open, read the note and stopped. Throwing the letter on the counter, she erupted in anger, "They can't - CAN NOT - do that!"

The Ryans, unbeknown to Clara, had taken pains to fill in every form handed to them by DOCS in their bid to be the guardians of Clara. Without explanation, the Ryans had been turned down.

But DOCs could and did. Clara was to be placed with a foster family further up the valley, away from town. The letter stated that Clara would continue with her schooling at Banjo Point High. The letter also stated that she was to be officially transferred from her present place of residence to her new family on Saturday week.

No one said anything. Each was stunned by such a decision being made with no face-to-face discussion.

Clara erupted, shaking, "Saturday - next Saturday! I'm going to my job at Pelican Point Clubhouse on Saturday. They will have to wait for me."

Clara was beyond angry. She was miserable. No information was forthcoming about her new so-called *family*. There was no logical reason as to why she could not stay with Lindy and her family.

The fateful Saturday arrived. When Clara returned from Pelican Point, Sam's car was parked outside Lindy's place. Clara clenched her jaw and ground her teeth; her hands forming fists.

Sam was waiting inside. When Clara entered, there she was - smiling as if Clara was a long-lost friend. Clara could only glare at her.

"Ms Successful Caseworker!" thought Clara.

Clara's fate was decided by this one person who had gained her trust and then, mistrust. Sadly, there was absolutely nothing Clara could do - she was a mere fifteen years old, and a ward of the state!

The atmosphere in the car was tense as Clara held onto her bitterness. It didn't bother Sam. She chatted as if the outcome could not have been better.

Clara's new accommodation was on a hill, a significant distance from the ocean, the river and the Sailing Club. It faced west, across the barren plains of the interior. The ground was dry and dusty.

Her foster parents - Dee and Archie - were warm and welcoming. As carers, they knew their role. They had expectations of Clara as a fifteen year old; expectations that included responsibilities such as helping with chores, and tending the vegetable garden as well as adherence to timelines.

Clara knew - instinctively - that she would not consider this as her home. She already felt she was here against her will for the next three or so years. And far too far from her special place - with Crusty on *Wave Leaper.* The foster carers accepted, a little begrudgingly, that Clara would continue to work at Pelican Point Sailing Club on Saturdays and race with Crusty on Wednesday evenings.

However, Clara lied to them when they asked how long the coaching and the Twilight Races would continue. All year she assured them, despite knowing the season was almost over. She conspired (at least in her head) to escape to Lindy's on Wednesday in the off season and do homework together. She would slip in to see Crusty each Wednesday afternoon. Maybe she could sail, instead of coaching, at Pelican Point on Saturdays.

Despite her efforts to accept her new situation, she found it embarrassing, especially since Billy was now labelling her as a DOCS kid; something he had slung out at her when she had again shown him up at school. The word had gone out.

*

In Clara's imagination, she would conjure up another life; a life where she was not being told what to do; where she was free to be who she was. YouTube had videos of people living on their boats; travelling the world whenever the mood took them. Clara dreamed of such a life and why not? She knew she was becoming more and more confident as a sailor.

*

Time drifted along. Clara was able to continue her guise as coach and sailor, enjoying Wednesdays with Crusty, and Lindy. On Saturdays, she would slip away to Pelican Point for a a badly needed sail. Therapy, she thought!

It was now August and the strong westerly winds covered the house on the hill with dust. As she walked up the hill from the school bus stop, she would watch the dust swirl around, a sense of smugness knowing that at least one afternoon a week she could get back to the Sailing Club. Spend some time with Crusty and *Wizz Kid.*

Walking along the gravelly road, she kicked at stones. Picking up a couple of them she threw one at a tree. That was for Mum. Another one whistled past the next tree - Dad! And the next one she slung at a fence - whack - Sam!

Her mobile pinged. It was Lindy. She sounded breathless.

"Crusty is sick. He's asking for you. Mumma says he's dying. I am so sorry, Clara. You need to get to the town hospital. Now! Dad is on his way to pick you up... are you at Dee and Archie's place?"

Clara started to melt down. Her top lip quivered. She could barely see the screen as she desperately tried to type a reply.

*

Lindy's dad sped down the dirt road from Dee and Archie's place, racing toward the town hospital.

With a sharp turn, he drove toward the *Emergency Area* and stopped. Clara jumped out and ran toward one of the nurses in Emergency. "Which room... which room... Crusty... uh... John Brenton?"

The nurse flipped through her file but, before she could let Clara know which room Crusty was in, Clara was already in flight.

"Room 337," the nurse shouted after her.

Taking the stairs three steps at a time, she was faster than the lift and in no time had made it to the third floor. She flew into Room 337 and there he was - her wonderful Crusty - propped up on a pillow, gazing out towards the ocean that he loved so much. Even his grey plait was laying out across the pillow, as if waiting patiently to be flicked around in excitement as it had so often done.

Without moving, Crusty knew Clara was there. In his gravelly voice, he asked, "That you, *yungun'*. I knew you'd come. I was waiting."

He turned his head toward Clara, eyes soft, trying to hold out his hand toward her, saying, "You, *yungun'*, are the daughter I never had."

Clara moved to his bedside, straightened her shoulders. She stood tall and strong, with her hands on her hips and grinned at Crusty, saying, "Well,

188

now, *oldun',* you are the best damn sailor I have ever known AND I've known a few, mate!"

They both grinned into each other's eyes. Clara then gently took his hand and together they looked out across to Henry's Bay and beyond; Clara working hard against her emotions.

A few moments later, Clara caved in.

"Don't leave me Crusty. I need you," she whimpered, her top lip quivering, tears streaming down her face. "I needed you in the past, but I also need you now and in the future. You cannot leave me now!"

Gently, Crusty squeezed her hand and said very slowly, faltering at times as he talked, "I'm not coming back. I'm done, but you - you have so much still to do. *Wave Leaper* is yours if you'd like her and I've left you some money, but you have to promise to sail her far. Sail her out into the deep dark blue ocean, until the land dips below the horizon. Sail to be free. Sail where no one tells you what to do."

"I don't know enough to sail *Wave Leaper* that far," Clara whispered.

"Yes, you do. You are the best damn sailor I've ever known."

He took a deep breath.

"I gave you all the lessons I could and you -

my daughter - you always listened. Go *yungun'*. Go and be free. I'm tired now. I need to rest."

"I'll stay 'til you wake again," Clara whispered, but then Crusty's grip loosened and the monitor beside his bed wailed a deathly monotone. He was gone, sailing over the horizon on a calm sea with a gentle breeze, dolphins breaking the surface near the bow, playing in the waves.

A movement behind her drew Clara back to the present. The heart beat monitor stopped its deathly wail as a nurse stepped in to switch it off.

"Won't be needing that anymore. He's gone. Surprised he held on so long. Kept asking for YUNGUN' and nobody knew who that was."

"I'm *yungun'*," Clara sad softy, "and Crusty was my very best friend!" Clara stood there, hunched, holding Crusty's hand.

Lindy's dad had moved into the room. He put his arm around Clara. She turned and wept into his shoulder, gulping air as she spoke, "He's gone and I didn't even know he was sick. He's gone. Crusty, my best friend in the whole world, is gone."

She turned to his lifeless body, weeping into his hand, "I'm so sorry, Crusty, so very sorry."

And then the nurse was closing his eyes with her finger tips, covering his face with a sheet; his plait all that remained visible.

It was time to leave.

*

The funeral was attended by a handful of people. Crusty was cremated; his ashes given to the Sailing Club to be thrown to the wind at a time when a westerly gale would whip up whitecaps across the Banjo River, taking his spirit home.

*

Clara, Peter and Lindy's dad had braved the conditions that special day in late August. The ashes flew out the moment the box's lid was opened, sucked away by the gale. As they returned to the Clubhouse, Clara was almost surprised to see *Wave Leaper* tugging at her mooring, rearing to go, wanting to be out there - wild and free with Crusty.

Clara walked to the end of the jetty.

In a calm confident voice she whispered, "Not now, *Wave Leaper,* not now. Wait for me. I'll be back."

TWENTY NINE

By September, the cold westerly gales had subsided. Clara knew that the Twilight Races would begin on the second Wednesday of the month. *Wave Leaper* would not be ready. She had not been to the Banjo Point Sailing Club since that August evening when they had released Crusty's ashes.

But Clara had a plan: one that she could not share with anybody. Yet! In fact, it was so secret that she had to work hard not to get too excited in case she blurted it out. She had indulged in enough YouTube videos on ocean sailing over the cooler winter months to the point of being all but ready to sail away. She had imagined over and over the idea of sailing out into the open ocean on *Wave Leaper* - Crusty's last request of her that sad afternoon. She could hear him, as if he was sitting right beside her, saying:

"Sail her out into the deep dark blue ocean, until the land dips below the horizon. Sail to be free. Sail where no one tells you what to do."

Where and with whom she would sail was more complicated. Whoever she chose to accompany her had to be told of the plan, accept the plan and keep it secret. Of course, Lindy was her first choice, but she probably needed at least one other.

Difficult times ahead she thought as she ambled towards the Sailing Club. She was focussed on checking that *Wave Leaper* did not 'feel' neglected over the past few weeks. She would board *Wave Leaper* and check over the systems for the upcoming Twilight Race Season. Charge the batteries. Check the fittings. Ensure *Wave Leaper* was shipshape. It's what Crusty would have wanted her to do. And, she had to admit, getting away from Dee and Archie had become a constant hunger.

Leaning back, pulling slowly on the oars, a sense of happiness surrounded her. The river was sparkling. Calm, almost serene. She was enjoying this moment. And then she stopped - both oars floating on top of the water. Her eyes grew wide. She could see clearly that something about *Wave Leaper* had changed. It was the rigging on the two masts. New! Every rope had been replaced. The hull had been cleaned. A fresh coat of antifouling paint covered the hull below the waterline.

Tying the dinghy to the stern of *Wave Leaper,* Clara scampered onboard. More surprises greeted her.

The sail covers were replaced with new beige coloured canvas. Sliding the hatch open, she knew that the cabin had recently been cleaned; the seat covers replaced and the floors covered with new carpets. Even the diesel tanks were full; the water tanks topped to the brim. It was clear that a new chart plotter had been installed above the chart table and, as Clara flicked through its menu, she found that Crusty had bought maps for every part of the world.

Wandering into the forward cabin, Clara stopped short. Every space was filled with canned goods; food that would no doubt feed her for a year. Clara was dumb-founded. Crusty must have organised this; paid for it in advance, knowing he wasn't even going to be there!

And all for Clara - for that she was now very sure. She could hear him again, whispering his last words, telling her that "*Wave Leaper* is yours if you'd like her."

Clara was stunned. She remembered those words but didn't realise what he really meant at the time. She remembered Crusty, on that fateful day, lying listless on the hospital bed, gazing out toward Henry's Bay. She had been focussed on Crusty - his face, his gentle eyes, his gaze directed on her.

"Don't worry, my best buddy, I will look after *Wave Leaper* - keep her maintained for you." She said out loud.

*

Friday was Clara's 16th birthday. There was no acknowledgement from either Archie and Dee when she was preparing for school that morning. She was withdrawn at school; keeping to herself for most of the day, emotions under control. As she climbed off the school bus and walked toward the 'dusty house on the hill', she could see a few letters sticking pout of the mailbox box at the end of the driveway. She pulled out the letters and noted one was addressed to her. She knew it was important. A lawyer's logo was obvious in the upper left hand corner of the envelope. Walking up the stony driveway, Clara opened her letter, and began reading:

"*Dear Ms Tage,*
    In the matter of the Will of John Brenton, better known as Crusty ..."

Clara began to tremble.

"*you have been identified as his sole heir and benefactor. You will have full ownership of his vessel, Wave Leaper, including all of its contents and accessories...*"

It hit her - hard. The upgrade of *Wave Leaper*.

"*Furthermore, a Trust Fund has been set up.*"

Clara was stunned. Crusty had left her a fortune! $1.8 million to be exact. In a Trust Fund! Peter, her team leader in the *Learn to Sail School*, was the Fund's Trustee.

Instead of bouncing with happiness, Clara placed her hands over her face and wept; gratitude overflowing as she gave quiet thanks to her Crusty. She reflected on the evening that she had swum toward *Wave Leaper* to help Crusty save her from those black, sharp rocks. It was over a year ago and now ... so much had happened.

As Clara entered the house, Dee called from the kitchen, "Clara, I need some eggs, please. Can you them from the henhouse?"

Clara *obeyed the order,* moving toward the henhouse; she could feel a change in her confidence. She had a plan! That secret plan! Now she had an official document to say she owned the boat and so much more.

She whispered to herself, "Happy 16th birthday, yungun'."

"Have you been crying again, missy?" Dee asked as Clara entered the kitchen, basket in hand. "You know, you really need to be more grateful. We have provided you with a wonderful home but all we get from you are tears! Doesn't make any sense to me. Have you finished your homework yet as I need some help in the kitchen. You need to peel the potatoes and what was that letter you got? Hope it's not more trouble!"

In typical Dee fashion, she continued on, asking one question after another. All communication ended with either a lecture or an instruction or both.

Clara smiled - her knowing smile, the one she always gave to Billy when he tried to put her down.

She steadied herself and remarked, "I'm grateful and no, I haven't finished my homework and yes, I can help you with the potatoes and the letter was of no consequence."

Clara had learnt that it was better to answer Dee in one string to avoid more questions. She headed to her room to finish her business assignment before returning to peel potatoes.

The following Wednesday, Clara met Lindy and Billy at the jetty. They were feeling energetic and certainly ready to rally for the first Twilight Race of the season. She was skipper now and knew the most about sailing *Wave Leaper*, but their help was undeniably crucial. Together they had a chance of doing well.

Billy and Lindy were impressed with the improvements. Apparently, all the work had been completed at Banjo River Marina, a small marina not far from the Clubhouse. They were an outfit who took great care in their workmanship, and it showed.

While surveying below deck, they entered the forward cabin. Billy groaned as he considered the mass of food in front of him.

"That's pretty stupid, you know. How are we supposed to race with half a ton of deadweight up front. Let's dump that before next week. These cans are probably all well past their expiry date. A bit like Crusty," he mocked.

Clara turned on Billy, a snarl on her upper lip, "Don't you **ever** say anything bad about Crusty **ever** again or I'll panel beat you, mate."

Billy knew she meant it, but as usual, had to have the last word, "Settle down, Princess. That red-headed temper and all those freckles are getting to y...."

He never finished the insult! Clara punched him, with ferocity, from behind, a single blow into his back. He never expected, nor saw it, coming.

He looked around, wounded; his eyes wild as Clara shook her hand. "That hurt," she said.

"Hurt me, too," grunted Billy, feeling better knowing that Clara was in pain as well.

"Whew, you don't punch like a girl."

"Is that a compliment or an insult, Billy? Watch out! and choose your words wisely. There's another where that came from. Mate!"

"Slow down, you guys. We have to work together. Happily! You know - WE. ARE. A. TEAM. And, there is a *lot* to do to get ready."

Lindy, always the logical one, separated the two, handing Billy a life jacket, "Get it on and get serious. WE need the sails up. *Now*!"

Removing the covers from the sails, Lindy and Billy gasped. New sails! Winching them upward, the sails crackled as they stretched along the spars. *Wave Leaper* was in better condition and had better equipment than she, without a doubt, had ever had. This was certainly a superior version of the old yacht.

A puff of warm wind rustled across the sails, making them billow out. Was that Crusty? Wishing them good luck?

Soon *Wave Leaper* was heading to the start line. She was alive. She was fast. She was in the hands of a capable crew. She would be hard to beat. And she was.

*

With all of the equipment stashed away, Billy was in a hurry to head home, but Clara and Lindy stayed on to enjoy a few minutes of quiet. Lindy handed Clara a small box, wrapped in a shimmering deep blue paper with a light blue ribbon.

She leaned over and gave Clara a hug, and then smiled, saying, "Happy 16th birthday, Skipper!"

Clara hugged Lindy back. Taking a deep breath, she looked Lindy in the eyes, saying, "Lindy, I have been thinking - a lot. *Wave Leaper* is now beautiful - no issues to worry about - and I... uh...

hmm... am the actual owner of her. A um... uh... a birthday gift from Crusty."

Lindy shook her head - confused.

Clara reached out and placed her hand on Lindy's shoulder.

Taking another deep breath, she continued, "It really is true, Lindy. A letter from Crusty's lawyer arrived last Friday. I am... well, I was shocked! I am his sole heir."

Lindy placed her hand over mouth, and then in one movement, swooped onto Clara with a mighty bear hug.

Clara gently pushed Lindy back and softly asked, "And so... what do you think of sailing her out into the ocean, across to some of the nearby islands or even New Zealand?"

Eyes round as a full moon, Lindy nodded, "Sounds good, but when and how and why and...", she began to chuckle, "are you serious?!"

Clara responded, slowly, carefully, "I just wanted to know if you would consider it. I'm thinking about it. Maybe the week after school is complete. And we will both be 16, by then!

"It's a big ask", commented Lindy, both hands turned upward, questioning. "What has brought this on, and... so soon. Are we ready? Able? Allowed? Where is this coming from?"

"Well, they say you only regret the things you didn't do and I've enough regrets in my life already."

"Yeah, but sailing into the ocean to far away islands or, as you say, New Zealand, could be a big mistake. Would we be permitted at sixteen? Even be considered too inexperienced," Lindy mused.

Clara rejoined, "You only get experience by doing things. You can't wait around and continue to learn, learn, learn. You have to jump in and experience what you know. Take Jessica Watson as an example. Around the world alone without stopping. Without support. I'm sure you and I together could venture out onto the ocean for awhile. Plus, *Wave Leaper* is bigger and more seaworthy, I suspect, than Watson's yacht."

Lindy's mobile pinged in the silence that now hung between them.

"It's Dad. I'm going to need to go. Can we give you a lift to the bus stop or drive you to your dusty home on the hill?"

"Either would be great. Hey, Lindy... let's just think about it, but the most important thing is... it's our secret. No-one else can know or the idea could totally unravel before it has even started."

Clara knew she could trust Lindy to keep this secret but would she come onboard? Would she be prepared to join Clara in this ocean experience?

At school the next day, Lindy gave Clara a wink; a covert thumbs up and Clara knew Lindy had decided to join her. The plan was coming together.

*

The following Tuesday, Clara made up a story for Dee about a fictitious event in the library she wanted to attend after school. Instead, she headed to *Wave Leaper,* pen and note pad in hand. Once on board, she scratched around in Crusty's chart table drawer, where he kept all of his paperwork. Crusty was decidedly meticulous and, in no time, she found what she was after. A list of all the cans of food, their expiry dates and which lockers they were placed in. Further digging around led her to a list of meals she could make, another list of dry packaged ingredients in the aft cabin, along with a list of long-life milk products, custard as well as cream, stored in the lockers under the settee. What was her greatest surprise was a list entitled **Menus for an Ocean Crossing.**

Crusty had undeniably, and ably, perfected Clara's plan. All Clara had to do was to buy fresh produce when the time came.

THIRTY

A sublime Saturday evening saw Lindy and Clara on board *Wave Leaper.* A sleepover! Lindy's folks were happy for such an arrangement, and, as far as Dee and Archie were concerned, Clara was spending the night with Lindy. Which she was!

They giggled over their plan to *escape;* a dream for the moment. But in reality, could they do it? They poured over the school atlas that Lindy had brought with her, and then used the chart plotter to calculate distances and the number of days a destination would take to reach.

Firstly, they'd have to sail far away from Australia, especially from DOCS to avoid Clara being sent back to Dee and Archie. Although New Caledonia was closest, Fiji and Tahiti and all the rest of French Polynesia enticed them.

"Imagine," Clara announced, with a straight face. "Palm-fringed atolls, living off coconuts and fresh fish 'til I'm 18."

And then she dissolved into laughter.

While the girls continued to pour over the atlas, questions kept popping up. What about passports? And documentation? What would they need in order to be permitted to moor in different countries? Would questions be asked of them?

The secret plan had flaws and the girls agreed that at this stage the *great escape* seemed improbable but this did not deter them. Their energy was unstoppable: their eyes sparkled with excitement as they giggled into the evening.

"Never give up," Clara beamed, and then gulped, a twinge of sadness spreading across her.

"Just maybe we should hold the thought. It's no use sailing the world only to stuff everything up. Bide our time, I think. Wait till the moment's right."

"What about we sail up the coast to Pelican Point in the holidays?" Lindy suggested, "It's only 40 nautical miles. Take us a day - long day - with a southerly behind us. Spend a few days in the area. Then get back on the first nor'easterly that comes up," suggested Lindy.

"Excellent idea. We could invite Billy along to test him out!" Clara replied, with just a hint of sarcasm.

They both knew that Billy was a good sailor; strong, resourceful. In the silence that followed the girls both wondered if they could trust him. Should they consider him for the big plan?

Lindy couldn't stop laughing, "Billy could be our chef. Test him out as a cook, chained in the galley."

Clara jumped up and, in her best pirate voice, uttered, "I'm the Skipper and this is my ship. I'll make him clean the bilges and walk the plank if he gives any cheek. He wouldn't even know we were testing him."

Eventually the hilarity of the thought of Billy being chained to the galley or cleaning out the bilges settled and Clara declared, "Ok, it's a deal, Lindy! Soon after the term ends, we'll watch for a good weather window and go when the time is right. I'll drop a hint to Billy and see if he's keen."

"We could load up with fresh fruit and veggies just before we go. I'm so excited. I'll tell Mum and Dad tomorrow. I'm sure they will agree, as long as we are careful. We will need to outline our plan in detail and I guess get it signed off.

Despite the laughter and hysteria, Clara knew that planning an adventure up the coast was a good start towards her escape plan. Despite seeming out of reach for the moment, Clara was confident that one day she would sail the open ocean.

She promised Crusty.

One day.

Summer holidays had begun. Billy had agreed, rather enthusiastically, to come along on the adventure. Both Billy's and Lindy's parents were in full agreement and, with thanks to the Ryans' intervention, Dee and Archie gave Clara a 'thumbs up'.

Clara, Billy and Lindy would be on the ocean soon, sailing *Wave Leaper* purely for enjoyment, if only for a few days.

On the first Sunday of the holidays, the girls motored *Wave Leaper* around to Banjo River Marina and topped up on diesel. At the moment, it looked like a good southerly would blow them up the coast on Tuesday. The countdown was on.

"Either she's sprung a leak or you've got a ton of stuff on board," the Marina's assistant, a bloke around twenty, grinned at the girls.

"She's down on the waterline a bit," he continued, trying to get a response from the girls as they stood beside *Wave Leaper* tied up alongside the fuel dock.

"Mighty fine vessel this. Old Crusty got us to go over her bow to stern during the winter. He didn't spare a cent; kept saying he was sailing out soon. Guess that's what he meant about dying, poor ol' bloke."

He hesitated before continuing, "Good that you girls are enjoying the Twilight Races on her," and then hooked the fuel hose back onto the bowser.

Clara thanked him, paid for the fuel and, as they gently puttered away, he called out, "Let me know if you ever want to sail onto the ocean. I'd be proud to come along."

Clara and Lindy's eyes met and there was a long discussion in that glance.

"We had thought of sailing to Tassie some time soon," Clara lied, "We'll keep you in mind."

THIRTY ONE

On Monday night, with *Wave Leaper's* dinghy now raised out of the water and lashed onto the foredeck, the three sailors settled into a comfortable night's sleep, in preparation for their early morning crossing of the sandbar, and out onto the ocean.

In the light grey and rising pink of dawn, relaxed, almost carefree, they rose, enjoyed their first breakfast on board, carefully, almost studiously, re-checking every piece of rigging, including the hull, sails, pumps, and engine, as well as the tool kit and spare parts were stored and secure. They then slipped the mooring to begin their adventure.

"Take a couple of seasick tablets, Billy. We don't want you spewing all over the place. The ones on the chart table are non-drowsy. Don't want you snoring on duty," Clara laughed, "Lindy and I have already taken a dose."

*

"Good. First waypoint passed," Clara murmured to herself as they passed the Banjo Point Lighthouse, heading out into the ocean. The plan was to motor straight out to sea until the southerly came in and then raise the sails to run before the wind along the coast. The ocean was glassy. A lazy swell gently lifted and dropped the hull as the yacht sliced though the water.

Just after 08:00 hours, the first signs of the southerly appeared, along with a bank of clouds that soon was skipping overhead as the cool wind punched through the calm air.

"Two reefs in the main and a bit of jib out. Let's see how she settles," Clara called as Lindy and Billy moved onto to the open deck to raise the main sail.

Promising their parents that they would be mindful of ensuring they were safe on board, they securely fastened their life jackets and snapped on their harnesses as they began to hoist the main sail.

Wave Leaper forged forward, alive and in her element; the young sailors confident in their abilities to sail her safely. The coast slid past and soon they could make out in the distance the headland that marked the entry into the bay where Pelican Point Sailing Club was nestled, tucked away from the ocean swells, and the strong southerly that carried them forward.

It was a glorious sail. Perfect, in fact. As the morning moved toward noon, Billy made some lunch: ham, tomato and cheese wraps. They munched on these while they monitored the sails and then, with ease, rounded the point and crossed the sandbar at the high tide. Then they tightened up the sails and began the two nautical miles up the bay before dropping anchor in the calm water just off the Pelican Point Sailing Club.

As soon as everything was stowed and *Wave Leaper* was shipshape, Clara dived into the clear water and followed the anchor chain along its length, checking that it was dug well into the sandy bottom.

Then it was time. They made a competition out of jumping off the bow, swimming around the boat, and being the first to climb back and over onto the deck.

Clara was living her dream. Sailing *Wave Leaper* onto the ocean, mooring behind comfortable headlands, relaxing with her two 'mates': having fun. Lindy caught a fish for their first holiday meal together but it had to be released back into the water - too small!

Billy, in the meantime, was checking Crusty's purchases. Tins of tomatoes, beans, soups, and even tuna. Billy considered the options. They had a good supply of fresh veggies and fruit so maybe a couple of tins of tuna might do for dinner.

They were a team at the moment, and as they settled in for the night, *Wave Leaper* gently rocked them to sleep; a more idyllic scene could not have been imagined.

As Clara drifted off to sleep she wondered if Crusty was looking down on their adventure with pride.

*

The sun sparkled in through the hatches and Lindy, being first up, headed to the wash basin where she encountered a problem.

She turned and called to Clara, "We've got no water. Nothing."

"Damn, I'll check the tanks... give me a moment."

Within minutes, Clara called back, "Empty, all gone, nothing left!"

"Greeeeat! Now what are we going to do?" groaned Billy.

"First, find the source of the leak and then we'll need to fill up!"

All three of them rummaged around, but, without some water in the tanks, finding the source of the leak was going to be tricky.

"Nothing for it, guys. We'll have to go ashore with a jerry can. Get some water from the Pelican Point Clubhouse. Fill up the various tanks. It's going to be a long day."

The problem, thankfully, was a simple one. A pipe had split below the sink and with the pumps turned on, all of the water had drained into the bilges.

The bilge pump had been efficient. Throughout the night, all their precious water had been sent overboard

"Ok, the lesson is..." Clara announced, "don't leave the pumps on and, if you hear a pump running, find out why. Got it?"

"Aye, aye, Captain," grinned Billy and Lindy, standing tall and saluting Clara as she faced them, hands on hips, shaking her head.

*

Calm had returned to *Wave Leaper* by mid-afternoon. A few of Clara's juniors from Pelican Point Sailing Club clambered onboard. They loved scrambling around the main deck, eyes wide and in awe of such a big boat. Below deck they saw where Clara and her sailing mates slept, and the place where they ate. Lindy offered them dinner on board but no - their parents were calling them ashore. Time to head home.

As the sun slowly sank into the western sky, Billy walked toward the saloon table. Lindy and Clara were listening to the weather forecast for the next twenty-four hours. Nor'easter was predicted for the next day.

Billy stretched his arms wide and pronounced, "Ok! Weather window looks good for tomorrow. Let's head back as soon as the nor'easter pipes up."

Lindy butted in, "Shush! Billy. There's more!"

Too late. The weatherman had moved on.

"Billy, you turkey, what if we missed something important. I heard something about an east coast low."

"Nah, Lindy, we'll be just fine. It's *summer* and the nor'easter will blow for a few days - the usual pattern. It's always the same in summer. Trust me - the next southerly will be through in a week or so."

Clara stepped in and saluted Billy, "Ok, Mr Weather Expert! Considering your sage advice, we will leave around 8ish and by 10:00 hours the nor'easter should kick in. Get us back to Banjo Point around 18:00 hours... In time for the high tide with the glow of sunset bearing us past the lighthouse."

"That was a bit poetic there, Princess," Billy laughed as he chewed on a piece of sourdough.

"Well, shiver me timbers, I have more for you....

Sunset and evening star,
And one clear call for me!
And may there be no moaning of the bar
When I put out to sea.

and that, my mates, is Shakespeare," grinned Clara as she gave a deep bow.
"Good one, Clara, but look at you. You look cold, time to don a jacket, Captain. It's cooler now," Lindy winked.

And in her best pirate voice, she advised the crew, "AARRGGGH, keep a weather eye open, me hearties!"

THIRTY TWO

The anchor chain clattered over the bow roller. Clara looked out across the bay: the surface a perfect mirror disturbed only by *Wave Leaper* bobbing around as she was being prepared for the trip home. A puff of black smoke hung around the stern; the exhaust spluttered in the water.

Soon *Wave Leaper* had rounded the point and was motoring across a glassy ocean, disturbed only by a lazy swell from the southerly that blew along the coastline a few days before. The nor'easter was to kick in around 09:00 hours.

"Lindy, text your mum, hey. Let her know we've left. Should be in around Banjo Point by 18:00 hours or earlier if the nor'easter comes through as predicted. Then we'll cross the bar on the high tide just after sunset and be moored, for sure, well before 20:00 hours. Hey Billy! Might be wise to message your parents as well. Ok?"

Around 09:00 hours, the nor'easter, as predicted, kicked in, gently at first before reaching

25 knots by mid-morning. The trip south to Banjo Point would be fun and fast.

The land was heating up and, further inland, puffy clouds could be seen rising above the ranges. A perfect day to sail home, back to Banjo Point.

And then things changed. Billy was confused to see cumulonimbus clouds beginning to build further south. Within minutes, the nor'easter had died out and *Wave Leaper* was becalmed.

"Billy, remember when you interrupted the weather report last night? I think we missed this change... are we in trouble?" called out Lindy.

And the answer came, not from Billy, but from the wind. The southerly had busted in and was steadily increasing in strength.

Wave Leaper plowed forward under full sail while the crew gathered in the cockpit to decide what to do next.

"OK, some options. We can't go back into Pelican Point Bay until it's high tide. That'll be just after dark. So we could hang around here and wait."

Clara looked around. Not much enthusiasm came from either Billy or Lindy.

"Alright, then, next two options. Stay close to shore and tack our way down the coast, *or* make one long tack out to sea and then another long tack back to Banjo Point in order to cross the bar just after dark."

"But," interrupted Lindy, "we need to know what's happening. Weather report on the marine radio - we really need to hear it. I think it's on at 10:00 hours and that's soon. So c'mon, let's listen in."

Right on 10:00 hours, the weather report began with "'Sécurité, sécurité, sécurité. All ships. A severe east coast low is developing."

The announcer went on to explain that the centre of the low was south of Banjo Point, and the low was deepening. Wind gusts could exceed 50 knots, with a rapidly developing swell to ten metres. Any vessel in the area should attempt to reach port as soon as possible."

It was expected that the upcoming storm cell would move slowly north and could possibly become more severe within the next twenty-four hours.

As the weather report finished, there was a long silence amongst the three. The severity of the situation was clear. They wouldn't be able to enter the safety of any bay until the high tide that evening. By then, the swell would be at such a level that crossing the sandbar would be near impossible, and, without a doubt, dangerous.

"Geez, Billy, this is *your* fault, you know," Clara grunted.

"I didn't cause the weather," growled Billy.

"Yeh? But we wouldn't have left if you had shut up yesterday! We would NEVER have left if we had known this was coming."

"Well, don't blame me. You should have checked the weather again before we left this morning, *Captain!*"

Lindy's dark eyes were wide with fear. The oncoming peril made her turn on Clara and Billy, as she exploded, "OK! Stop blaming each other. We need a plan. Let's get our act together. We are supposed to be a team!"

"You're right Lindy, but Billy, you were wrong with your wise words last night. We ARE in trouble," and as her freckles began to redden, she moaned, "But I guess - yes - we - I - should have checked the weather before we moved off."

"But now, we have no options, except to handle the next few hours as best we can," and with that, they gave each other a *high five* and went to work.

And, as if waiting for the cue, a stronger gust whipped up the surface of the sea, laying *Wave Leaper* over. It was clear to each of them that it was time to reef down the sails and prepare for a storm. With two reefs in the main, the mizzen packed away and the jib furled, *Wave Leaper* settled into a comfortable motion.

And then Clara made a decision. The safest option was to head further north, out to sea, avoiding the dangers of the coastline by sailing around the far side of the low. Having few options left, agreement was reached; sea sick tablets were taken, water bottles prepared, snacks brought up into the cockpit and the hatches battened down.

Clara remembered Crusty saying "handle 50 knots and 40 is easy", but she had another sort of knot in her stomach. As she hugged her stomach, she was aware that the crests of the waves had become whitecaps as far as the eye could see.

Wave Leaper was down to her storm jib. With only a tiny bit of mainsail by mid-afternoon, she bounded over each wave and down into the next trough at 8 knots. The ocean was breaking all around her, gushing down the side decks. Spray filled the air, and rain poured down in sheets.

Around 17:30 hours, Billy volunteered to put the last remaining part of the mainsail away. Clara and Lindy watched Billy through the spray dodger.

It was difficult work, trying to hold on while tying the flapping sail down. All the while, waves broke around him. The girls watched in horror.

Twice he was washed off his feet, landing against the mast. His tether held and, after what seemed an eternity, he started to edge back along the deck towards the cockpit.

The wind was screeching through the rigging; the wind speed meter was recording a steady 55 knots, gusting to 60. Billy tumbled into the cockpit; his wet weather gear sloshing water onto the deck as he managed to sit upright.

Nature's angry conversation had Billy shouting to be heard, "That was hectic. I thought I was going over the side and, well, there was no way you could turn around and pick me up. I would have been a goner."

Clara turned toward Billy, her knuckles white on the wheel as she tried to hold *Wave Leaper* on a course away from the east coast low.

"Well done Billy, I'm glad you're here, MATE! Big thanks."

THIRTY THREE

By nightfall, *Wave Leaper's* crew was exhausted. Not trusting the autopilot, Lindy and Clara took turns at the wheel while Billy tinkered with the mechanism. Finally, Billy said that it was ready.

He slipped the belt onto the motor and adjusted the display to set the course. It had to work if they were to survive the night. Carefully releasing the wheel, Billy held his breath. Lindy and Clara stood facing him; fingers held high, crossed.

The electric motor moaned as it took up the challenge. The autopilot was spinning the wheel back and forth, keeping *Wave Leaper* on course as she rode up and down the waves.

"It seems to be holding a reasonable course," Billy shouted. "Why don't you two go below and have a rest. I'll keep watch up here."

"No way can you be on the shift alone, Billy," and turning to Lindy, Clara raised her hand, "Lindy, you head below. We'll swap out in a few hours."

Lindy needed no second invitation, sliding the hatch closed behind her just moments later.

The ocean around *Wave Leaper* became frightening. Following seas, driven by the wind, growled and snarled, approaching her from behind. White water in the darkness! Every third or fourth wave would crash onto her aft deck, threatening to break her to bits: to sink her.

Slowly, Wave Leaper would rise up in defiance; tons of water pouring back into the ocean. Then just as she was back on top, another wave would crash onto the deck, pushing her down.

The seas continued to break over the yacht. Suddenly a huge one flooded the cockpit. *Wave Leaper* seemed to stagger for much longer under the weight. In the shadowy darkness, Billy and Clara stared in horror but, in time, ever so slowly, *Wave Leaper* would rise again as the tons of water drained away. .

It was going to be a long night. The storm had caught up to them and they were alone. There was nowhere to go. No one could help. They couldn't escape.

Clara huddled under the spray dodger, her knees up against her chest to keep warm. She could hear the breaking waves approaching. The autopilot moaning. The wind, screaming through the rigging.

And then she thought she heard him. Crusty!

In her mind, she could hear his gravelly voice reminding her that, "to survive a big storm you need to place the boat in 'hove to'. And *yungun'*, you'll need a touch of mizzen to drive her forward. A bit of a backed jib to slow her down. She'll sit like a happy duck whatever gets thrown at her."

Clara jumped up, eyes wide. She knew what had to be done!

She shouted across to Billy, "Hey, liven up. I know what we need to do. Put *Wave Leaper* into 'hove to'. We need a hanky of mizzen sail out and then back the jib."

"Seriously, Clara... who's going to do *that* in the dark. Count me out. I did the main earlier and thought I was going to die. You do it."

Clara turned from Billy, muttering "selfish boy", as she shouted back, "Turn on the deck light. I can do this."

Clipping her harness tether onto the jack-line, she waited for Billy. As soon as the light beamed down from the cross trees of the mast, she bounded out from the safety of the cockpit to raise the mizzen.

Hanging on to the mast, the boat wild beneath her, she released the sail from the bag and began hoisting it upward. The mizzen was going to be a challenge with the wind at this strength. As she began to crank on the winch, a wave broke over the stern. She was now surrounded by white water. She hung on tightly. She could feel her fear rising as the water cascaded around her.

In her mind's eye, she could clearly see Crusty raising and lowering and raising and lowering the mizzen that day, so long ago, when Clara was supposed to be concentrating during the *Learn to Sail School*.

She could do this. She knew Crusty had set this scene up perfectly - for her.

The halyard creaked tight. A rogue wave roared in from the darkness. Again, she held on as tightly as she could. The water crashed into her, seeming to grab at her wet weather gear, working hard to wash her into the ocean.

A hanky of mizzen was shaking wildly. The winch handle was back in its pocket. Clara jumped back into the cockpit. She pulled on the sheet and the mizzen was under control.

"There you go, Billy, now we need to back the jib. C'mon. We need to work together. I'll crank it on this side as you ease the jib out. Wait... sorry... wait. Before we start, disengage the autopilot. Whoa - not so fast... we don't want the jib flapping. It'll tear in these conditions. Great. Perfect. We're good to go, Billy!"

Despite Billy's mumbling, he was following orders, and as Clara cranked on the jib, *Wave Leaper* slowly came up into the wind and stopped. Suddenly, she was calm, notwithstanding the wind still howling, and the rigging whistling. The waves were definitely parting as each one approached the bow, gently slipping beneath *Wave Leaper's* keel.

Clara grinned, "That's why Crusty was such a hero. I was just such a fool for taking so long to remember his instructions."

"Not bad, Clara, not bad," Billy turned to her, a high five ready!

Lindy poked her head out of the hatch. "What happened? Um... where did the waves go."

*

Wave Leaper's crew peered out into the darkness through the driving rain and spray. The wind howled and the rigging whistled but the threatening waves were broken by *Wave Leaper's* wake as she slipped sideways. Although *Wave Leaper* was calm, the storm, raging around them, was far from over.

"No need for the autopilot. I'll lash the helm and watch to make sure she's OK," shouted Clara above the wind, "I'll take the first watch till midnight and then it's yours, Lindy. Billy you're on at 04:00 hours."

Clara snuggled in under the spray dodger once the others had gone below. Looking out she waved, a self-conscious wave; the sort of wave when you wave to a friend, but you aren't sure if they're watching. She waved to Crusty hoping he was watching; hoping he was proud of Clara and her crew.

She admitted to herself that she had been afraid. Thought that they might not come out of the storm safely.

And now - she knew they would survive!

THIRTY FOUR

Finally, the dawn greyed the sky. Billy, exhausted, climbed down the companionway, and over to Lindy, giving her a shake, as he quietly said, "Rise and shine. Your shift, Lindy."

He could see Clara shifting in her sleep as he moved towards his bunk.

"Couldn't get much worse," Lindy yawned, "We are sure to be OK now. We're doing pretty good, overall."

Billy stretched and then collapsed onto his bunk in his wet weather gear, pulling his sleeping bag over himself, waving to Lindy, and mouthing, "All yours, Lindy."

Lindy stumbled into the cockpit. All she could see was white water and driving rain and spray. *Wave Leaper* continued to ride out the storm, as calmly as any boat could under gale force conditions.

She settled into a corner of the cockpit, up against the spray dodger; her arms folded in defence, trying to keep warm. Her eyelids became heavy and in no time she was also asleep. Wave Leaper was in charge!

After twenty-four hours, no one had eaten more than a few sweet biscuits. No one had slept more than a few tormented hours.

Lindy woke with a start. She wasn't sure of the time, but the wind had increased while she had dozed off.

The wind speed meter was steadily on 60 knots, now gusting to 65.

Quietly, Lindy slid the hatch open and went below. The cabin was damp, the air thick, but it was warmer and dryer than the cockpit. Slipping onto the chart table seat, Lindy could see the slow northward track on the plotter made by *Wave Leaper.*

She realised that it was now 09:25 hours and that she had all but slept through, not only her watch, but Clara's.

She decided, wisely, to wait till 10:00 hours before waking Clara.

*

As the wind howled across the rigging, a halyard continued to clang against the mast. Despite the storm raging around them, *Wave Leaper's* crew continued their two hour duty, collapsing onto their bunks when their vigil came to an end. Oblivious of their drenched wet weather gear, they drifted in and out of a restless sleep.

*

By mid-afternoon, Lindy was back on duty when a deep and controlled voice filled the cabin: a voice so calm - so out of place - in the raging storm.

Billy stirred. Clara was already sitting bolt upright.

"*Wave Leaper, Wave Leaper.* This is Australian Airforce *Orion.* Do you copy? Over."

Clara dashed across the cabin as Lindy made room for her behind the chart table. Grabbing the handset and forgetting all protocols, Clara's words tumbled out over the airways.

"Yes. Can you see us? We're here. Over."

"*Wave Leaper, Wave Leaper*, we have you visual. You look to be OK. How's it on board?"

"*Orion*, all three of us are safe. Alive and... uh...," she hesitated, "it's been pretty tough."

But in that moment, in that answer, Clara smiled, aware that she was the *Captain* and together they, as young sailors in their 'trial ocean sail', had sailed through a notorious east coast low.

"*Wave Leaper,* I see that you are 'hove to' and riding out the storm very well."

"*Orion*, we had a rough day yesterday. Only settled into 'hove to' after dark. Since then, we have been calm and comfortable."

"*Wave Leaper.* There has been concern for your safety. We will let your parents know that you are in a good position to make it on your own. No need for assistance? Are you OK with that?"

Clara hesitated and looked across to Billy.

"OK?" she asked.

"Wait a minute, some think time needed," insisted Lindy. "How long will we be riding out this storm? We need to work out where we are, and where we are we going?"

"Roger that," agreed Clara, and spoke into the handset, "*Orion*, what's the weather prediction? How long is this going to carry on for?"

"*Wave Leaper.* The storm is expected to be over by tomorrow - early morning - around 08:00 hours. The swell will take a few days to dissipate. We suggest you head north to Elizabeth Reef; anchor there. Take shelter and think about the next step."

"*Orion.* Roger that. Standby while we plot a course."

Clara zoomed into the plotter's screen and quickly identified Elizabeth Reef. She dropped a pin onto it. The distance popped up - 60 nautical miles.

Clara looked toward her crew. "If this settles down tomorrow, we can easily get there by midday. Maybe a bit later."

"Probably our best option," Billy concurred.

"I agree, as well," chimed in Lindy, "Let's head there. Secure *Wave Leaper* and give ourselves some thinking time.

"*Orion.* Heading to Elizabeth Reef seems to be a good option. As things calm down, we should anchor somewhere near the reef tomorrow around midday or thereabouts."

"*Wave Leaper*. There is a safe anchorage on the northern tip. A number of yachts are already sheltering there. We'll buzz over them and let them know when to expect you. We'll be doing another patrol tomorrow mid-morning so will check up on you then. Good luck. Standing by Channel 16."

"Standing by 16," answered Clara.

And with that, the Orion was gone, but not before taking photographs of the yacht, a tiny speck on a troubled sea; the surface of the ocean white with foam as waves broke around *Wave Leaper*.

The dramatic images were quickly circulated

across the world, on the front pages of newspapers, and across social media, with the headline '*Kids Lost at Sea in Mighty Storm*'.

Clara, Lindy and Billy breathed deeply in unison, high-fived each other, and prepared themselves for another uncomfortable night of riding out the storm. They reviewed the charts, considered timings and by mid-evening, were comfortable with their decisions.

A sense of relief had came over the crew. They could see an end to this ordeal.

By 21:00 hours, the wind was clearly dying down, although the waves were still angry, surging past *Wave Leaper* as she sat 'hove to'.

Although it was late, the crew suddenly became aware of how hungry they were. They needed food. Real food, not snacks.

"The best comfort food after a storm is… ," laughed Lindy, "egg and bacon omelette! Of course! Why? Goes down easily and, hopefully, stays down."

In no time the cabin was filled with the warm smell of eggs and crackling bacon. The pan swung back and forth on the gimballed stove, keeping level as the boat rocked from side to side. Holding on and stirring at the same time was difficult.

They ate heartily, wolfing down every morsel. Billy raised an eyebrow as he looked at the girls; then rose. Wedging himself into the galley, he began making a second round of omelettes! Again, not even a tiny piece of cooked bacon fat was left.

Giving kudos to both Lindy and Billy, Clara stood up and patted her belly as Billy burped loudly, "Almost human again, I'd say. Time for a change of clothes and a good sleep - fingers crossed - tomorrow it will be all over."

Night watches were cancelled as they were in the middle of nowhere and far from any shipping lane. The three shipmates knew that *Wave Leaper* would look after them as she rode out the remainder of the storm: her mizzen pushing her forward; the jib pushing her back.

Slowly she slipped downwind, making a wake that broke the coming waves, giving her a calmer ocean to ride through.

THIRTY FIVE

The Australian Airforce *Orion* buzzed over *Wave Leaper* earlier than originally planned, keen to check the yacht's progress. With the wind calmer, *Wave Leaper* was sailing strongly under full sail. As *Orion* passed over her, little did *Wave Leaper's* crew know that the Airforce was once again taking photos of the yacht leant into the surging waves and fresh winds.

As *Wave Leaper* sailed north toward Elizabeth Reef, the *Orion* continued on its circuit; its personnel feeling confident and assured that the young sailors would find secure anchorage soon.

*

Elizabeth Reef could only be seen at low tide when the wrecks on her coral shores become exposed. The rest of the time the fringing reef was below the surface. Only the white breaking waves protected the smooth blue lagoon. There was no island - no tropical palm trees rustling in the wind - just a languid lagoon.

Despite being several nautical miles from the atoll, the crew of *Wave Leaper* could clearly see one of the wrecks: a rusty fishing boat resting on the surrounding coral.

Keeping a safe distance from the pounding waves, they sailed towards the anchorage on the northern point of the reef; a place where the huge waves had beaten out their energy on the reef, leaving a safe harbour in its wake. Three other yachts were moored in this safe haven, sheltering from the swell.

As Clara looked for a sandy patch in which to lower the anchor, she manoeuvred *Wave Leaper* in amongst the other vessels. The water was crystalline. They could see the sand below and, although concerned that *Wave Leaper* might touch the bottom, the depth sounder registered a safe four metres. Over a patch of white sand, Lindy and Billy dropped the anchor. The constant roar from the surf reminded them of how safe they now were.

Wave Leaper came to rest. Clara breathed deeply.

Together, Lindy, Billy, and Clara had ridden out a major storm. *Wave Leaper* had looked after them but Clara knew, with certainty, that they survived because of Crusty. They had survived because of his careful and methodical lessons during those wonderful Twilight Races, including his meticulous preparation of his yacht.

In no time, the sailors from the other yachts paddled over in their dinghies and boarded *Wave Leaper*. They were all chattering at once, shaking the young sailors hands, clapping them on the back; congratulating them. They had heard the story of the kids lost at sea during the recent east coast low. All vessels had been asked to be on the lookout for them and here these heroes were - safe at Elizabeth Reef.

The sailors, settling around *Wave Leaper's* cockpit, were keen to hear the full story! The wanted to know all about the storm: the intensity of the wind, the waves, how *Wave Leaper* handled the extreme conditions. Did the yacht get swamped? Did she capsize at all? Was there any damage?

It became clear that these yachtsmen were indeed very experienced sailors, having sailed in many parts of the world - across the Atlantic, the Pacific - yet none had experienced an east coast low. They were clearly very impressed with these '*younguns*'.

Sensitive to the journey these young sailors had just experienced, the other sailors began to disembark to enable Billy, Lindy and Clara a chance to have a well deserved afternoon nap.

Later in the afternoon, the calm was disturbed by a float 'plane from the Lord Howe Island Police. As it touched down in the lagoon, it noisily taxied in close to the yachts. A dinghy collected a robust man with a bushy beard and rowed him across to *Wave Leaper.*

Once onboard, the policeman introduced himself as Inspector Clarens. He shook the young sailors' hands in a bearlike grip and congratulated them on their survival.

"That was a big storm over the last few days. Quite a bit of damage on Lord Howe. I'd hate to have been at sea!"

All three of *Wave Leaper's* crew winked at each other, standing tall together, proud of their teamwork.

Clarens had official questions to ask, but he already knew all the answers. These young sailors were not running away. He knew that their parents were aware of their sailing trip.

The Inspector then handed his 'sat phone' to Billy, "I spoke to your dad this morning and promised that you would ring once we connected. I've already established a signal and put in the code.

Dial your home number. He's waiting to hear from you."

Billy looked uncomfortable, handling the 'sat phone' as if it was poisonous.

"Do I have to? My Dad... uh... it may not be pleasant."

The girls knew Billy was nervous, and Lindy, arm across Billy's shoulder, offered assurance, "Come on, Billy, I'm next."

Hesitantly, Billy dialled his home number.

Almost immediately, he heard the receiver picking up and he quickly chirped, "Hi Dad. We're safe."

No sooner had Billy made his comment when a long, angry tirade erupted. All could hear his Dad 's rush of fury - of vitriol.

"I am so utterly disappointed in you! How can **I** hold my head up high around here! Sailing into an east coast low! As if you didn't know the consequences. What were you thinking. You are grounded... "

"But Dad... "

"Don't interrupt me, boy. Grounded for the entire summer holiday. Do you have any idea of the pandemonium you have caused around here. You! And... and.. those two other delinquents you are with! None of this should have ever happened. On the news, no less! Your mother was sick with worry - still is! Just wait 'til I get hold of you. I had hoped you would make **ME** proud!"

And with that the phone clicked dead. Billy slowly looked up, stuttering, "Guess that didn't go too... um ... uh... well."

"Pretty soul destroying, mate, but I'd be proud of what you and the girls have done," Clarens nodded.

Inspector Clarens handed Lindy the 'sat phone', "Your turn, Lindy."

And with that, he quietly noted, "Hope it goes better than what just transpired for Billy."

With trepidation, Lindy dialled home. Only the waves breaking on the reef broke the silence.

"Is that you, Lindy?" Lindy could hear her mum trembling as she continued, "I'm so proud of you. I'm so proud of what you have managed. I was always confident you would be capable and reliable. I can't wait to give you a big hug. Hold on! Dad's here and pushing in."

"Lindy - my hero. I'm so impressed. I can't wait to hear all the stories, but best I hand you back to mum. So... so... so... proud of you."

As the call finally ended, Lindy looked across to Billy, with a gentle 'I'm sorry' expression. And that was all that was needed to be said. Billy mouthed back to Lindy a thank you.

The Inspector informed Clara that there was no need to contact Dee and Archie. They were just happy to know that she was safe.

A whirring directly above *Wave Leaper* signalled another float 'plane preparing to land. As it lumbered across to where the yachts were moored, it became obvious. A camera could be seen up against one of the 'plane's windows - the media had landed!

Soon a journalist and photographer carefully climbed out onto the 'plane's float as it came to rest. Waving their arms for someone to pick them up, they were obviously keen to ask a myriad of questions and to take photos. With authority, they boarded *Wave Leaper* and all but took over.

"Stand here for a photo. No, closer together. Clara? You need a Captain's hat. What were the waves like? I believe you didn't plan to go to sea. Are you still friends?"

The media team quickly returned to the float 'plane; their story ready to beam across the world.

Calm returned onboard *Wave Leaper*. Inspector Clarens wished the crew a good evening and, finally, Clara, Lindy and Billy were alone.

It had been a very long day.

THIRTY SIX

By noon the next day another float 'plane skimmed across the clear bright waters of the lagoon. As Inspector Clarens had explained to the young sailors, a support crew from the Banjo River Sailing Club would fly out to help sail *Wave Leaper* home.

Billy's dad, still grumpy as an old bulldog, but calmer, was prepared to acknowledge what these young sailors had accomplished. He, along with both Lindy's and Sandy's dads, including the young man from the Banjo River Marina as well as Peter, the team leader for the *Learn to Sail School* and Clara's Trustee, clambered into the waiting dinghy and rowed across to *Wave Leaper*. It was going to be a full crew onboard *Wave Leaper* for the long sail back to Banjo Point.

Together they worked to prepare *Wave Leaper* for the journey back to Banjo Point Sailing Club and, despite having sailed through a major east coast low only two days prior, by 19:00 hours, she was shipshape for the journey home the next morning. Eating their dinner on the deck, all seven of the crew were relaxed as they enjoyed the serenity of Elizabeth Reef, the sun setting over a lumpy sea in the distance.

The next morning, as the sun made a golden pathway across the calm waters of the lagoon, they weighed anchor, waved goodbye to the sailors standing on their yachts 'saluting' them, and set a course for Banjo Point Lighthouse, three hundred nautical miles south.

*

Three days later, *Wave Leaper* nudged alongside the wharf in front of the Club. It was mid-afternoon. Billy, Lindy and Clara stood side by side at the bow as a throng cheered and clapped.

Welcome home balloons, tied to the wrists of an eager and excited tribe of kids, floated above the crowd: Clara recognised some of the kids from the learn to sail classes and even some from Pelican Point Sailing Club. A few of her teachers and, surprisingly, some of Mum's colleagues from the Post Office were also in the crowd.

With *Wave Leaper* tied up alongside the wharf, they disembarked and headed toward the Clubhouse.

There was a sense of organised chaos! Someone was shouting three cheers. A loud hail of cheering burst forth and just at that point, some of their mates from school, guitars in hand, began strumming 'We are sailing! We are sailing'.

With no need for a prompt, the crowd joined in, singing,

>*'We are sailing,*
>*We are sailing,*
>*Home again*
>*'Cross the sea.*
>*We are sailing*
>*Stormy waters,*
>*To be near you*
>*To be free.*

As the song came to its end, the crowd finished with an even louder burst of, *'To be free'*, repeated over and over.

Clara spotted a satellite dish that had been set up and, at the end of a long cable, a TV camera pointed at a presenter holding a microphone and chatting to an invisible audience. A would be politician was strutting around trying to get noticed.

As the three young sailors began crossing the car park toward the Clubhouse, they were hoisted onto shoulders. Once inside, they were set down in front of the Mayor, formally dressed in his gown with the heavy gold chain draped over his neck. Microphone in hand, the Mayor cleared his throat loudly, as the throng filled the club and then he began:

"It is my privilege and pleasure to welcome these three brave young sailors home today… "

Clara looked up at the Honour Boards as the Mayor bumbled on about youth and the future and how proud the community of Banjo Point was of its young people.

Clara turned her focus toward the Gremlin Board to read Crusty's name, John Brenton. This was his day. He'd made it all happen. She found it just as the microphone was placed into her hand. Clara looked across at the expectant faces, and sucked in her breath, saying quietly to herself, "This is for you, Crusty".

"Thanks for being here today to welcome us home. It was rough, and we probably should have made different decisions. But we survived and, thanks to additional crew, we have happily returned to the best sailing club in the world."

The crowd cheered and clapped and whistled their delight. When calm returned, Clara, shuffling her feet, stared directly at the light fitting above her head, and then continued:

"Without Lindy and Billy beside me, this homecoming would not have happened. Many of you know that Billy and I have been arch rivals for a couple of years and Lindy and I are best friends. Together, we sailed through that storm, despite seasickness and chilling fear. We were incredibly tired.

Together we trimmed the sails, and stood on watch throughout the night when we thought every coming wave was going to capsize the boat and drown us.

We three Banjo Point sailors did it - together."

She hesitated and an anticipatory silence hung over the Clubhouse.

"But the real hero of this story is… John Brenton - our beloved Crusty. He was my mentor,

my hero and my best friend. Wave Leaper was his boat and so, in many ways, Crusty was always with us. He prepared Wave Leaper for every possible situation at sea. He prepared all three of us - as sailors - over the past year. He was - no - IS - Wizz Kid."

She paused, took a deep breath, and then continued,

"I only wish he could have been with us, I miss him very much.
Crusty asked me to sail Wave Leaper out to where the ocean was a deep blue and I guess we did it for him and, for now, we have fulfilled part of his wish."

The crowd clapped respectfully. And then some started singing 'We are sailing, We are sailing' and without hesitation the rest of the crowd joined in shouting the refrain 'to be free'.

Clara, her vision beginning to blur, handed the microphone back to the mayor.

Again, there was clapping and cheering. Clara scanned the faces, hoping to see her Mum, but she wasn't there.

She caught a glimpse of Sam standing near the door. It was as if a hand was reaching into her chest and squeezing her heart; a cold hand, taking her breath away. She wanted to run; to jump off the end of the wharf and swim away as she had done before. Instead, she looked at her bare feet, hoping that she was wrong. She did not dare to look in that direction again. Why would Sam be there, anyway!

And then she was being hugged. Someone was hugging her and, when she tried to look up, all she could see was a piece of paper waving in her face. As she straightened, she recognised Lindy's mother, June, smiling excitedly at her.

"We've got custody, Clara. You are going to live with us. No more trips over the hill away from the Banjo River. Lindy has a sister and you, Clara, are coming to live with us for as long as you wish."

Lindy and Tim joined in the hug, laughing and crying altogether. Clara looked across to where Sam had been standing near the door, just catching a glimpse of her t-shirt as she had turned to leave.

Peter handed Clara *Wave Leaper's* keys.

"She's back on her mooring. She's waiting for you there," he hesitated, "ready for another adventure."

And winked.

The idea of sailing *Wave Leaper* to distant lands could not have been further from her thoughts at that moment.

For now, she had come home.

She was free.

Manufactured by Amazon.com.au
Sydney, New South Wales, Australia